CO-042 S

CHINCHILLAS

A COMPLETE INTRODUCTION

Chinchillas are known for their beautiful and thick fur. Those with standard gray colored coats are most commonly seen in pet shops.

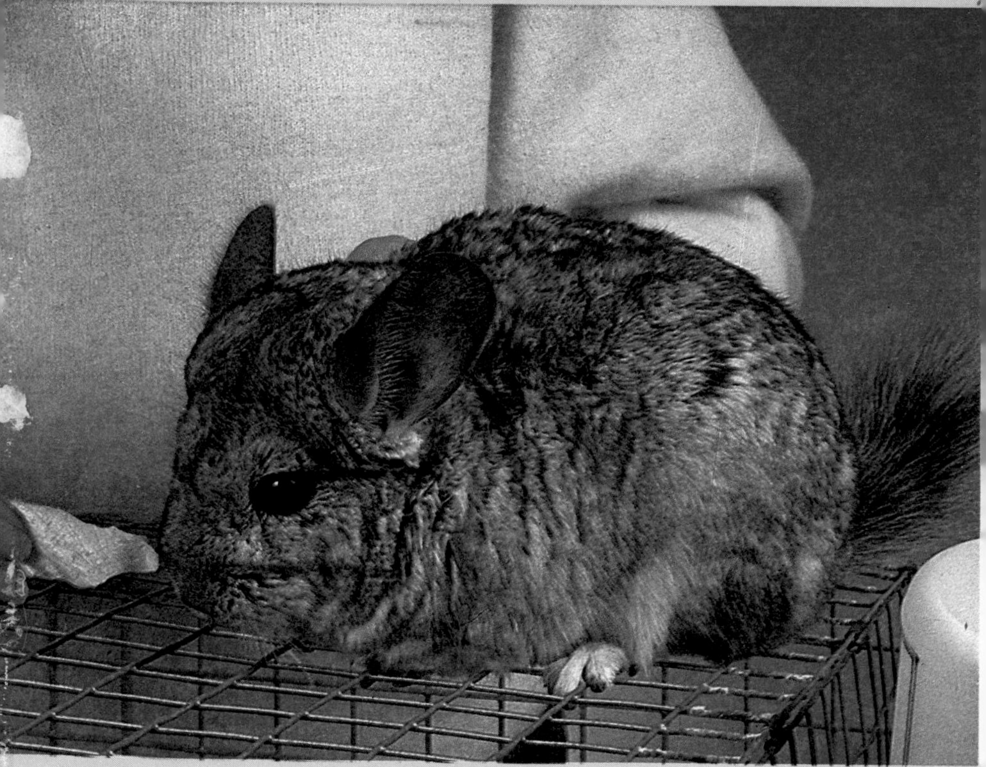

t.f.h.

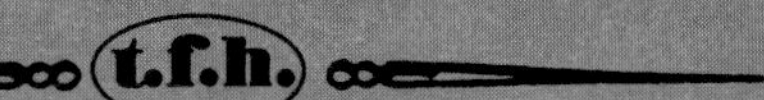

CHINCHILLAS

A COMPLETE INTRODUCTION

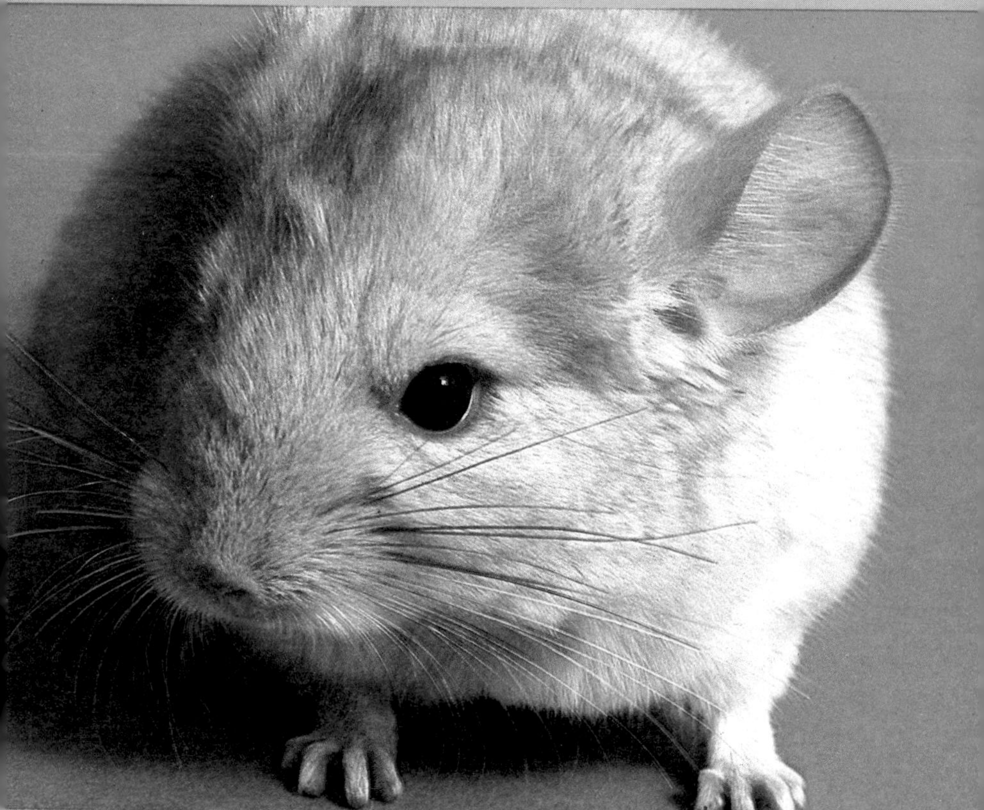

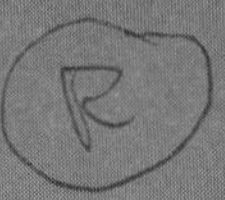

Photography: Dr. Herbert R. Axelrod, Michael Gilroy, Vince Serbin, J. A. Wilkinson (Valan Photos), and John Zeinert. Color drawings by John R. Quinn.

Distributed in the UNITED STATES by T.F.H. Publications, Inc., 211 West Sylvania Avenue, Neptune City, NJ 07753; in CANADA to the Book Trade by Macmillan of Canada (A Division of Canada Publishing Corporation), 164 Commander Boulevard, Agincourt, Ontario M1S 3C7; in ENGLAND by T.F.H. Publications Limited, 4 Kier Park, Ascot, Berkshire SL5 7DS; in AUSTRALIA AND THE SOUTH PACIFIC by T.F.H. (Australia) Pty. Ltd., Box 149, Brookvale 2100 N.S.W., Australia; in NEW ZEALAND by Ross Haines & Son, Ltd., 18 Monmouth Street, Grey Lynn, Auckland 2, New Zealand; in SINGAPORE AND MALAYSIA by MPH Distributors (S) Pte., Ltd., 601 Sims Drive, #03/07/21, Singapore 1438; in the PHILIPPINES by Bio-Research, 5 Lippay Street, San Lorenzo Village, Makati Rizal; in SOUTH AFRICA by Multipet Pty. Ltd., 30 Turners Avenue, Durban 4001. Published by T.F.H. Publications, Inc. Manufactured in the United States of America by T.F.H. Publications, Inc.

Contents

Your Chinchilla as a Pet

If you are reading this, you have either decided to have a chinchilla as a pet, or you are seriously thinking about taking on the responsibility of caring for one of these beautiful and unique animals. If the former is true, then this volume will aid you in learning about and taking care of your new charge. If the latter is the case, then this book will serve to illustrate the advantages (and possible disadvantages) of owning and caring for a chinchilla.

While a chinchilla can be educational and enjoyable as a pet for children, an adult should supervise the care and feeding of their chinchilla.

The decision to care for a pet is an important one. It requires a commitment on the owner's part to be accountable for another life. While other domesticated animals, such as dogs and cats, often have the run of a house and can be left on their own for long periods, small caged animals like chinchillas can not. A chinchilla requires much more attention, often on a daily basis. At first, purchasing a chinchilla for a child might appear to be an excellent idea, providing a youngster with a tiny, furry living plaything. But the exacting care chinchillas require demands responsible adult supervision. If you are obtaining a chinchilla as a pet for a child, then your commitment must extend to instructing the young owner of the importance of proper care. This book will serve as such an instructional volume.

Chinchillas are, of course, known primarily for their luxurious blue–gray fur. They are bred throughout the United States for their pelts, which are used for making extremely expensive fur coats and other extravagant garments. There are well over 3,000 chinchilla ranches in the United States and a population of close to 1,000,000 chinchillas, but the animal remains exotic and mysterious in the average person's mind. While familiar with the animal's fur-bearing reputation, the public appears largely uninformed regarding the animal's qualifications as a pet. However, this exotic attitude toward the animals is one of the very things that makes them increasingly desirable as pets.

Facing page: *Before you purchase a chinchilla for a pet, acquaint yourself with the one you intend to get by judging its temperament when handled. Full-grown adults are set in their ways and may resist handling.*

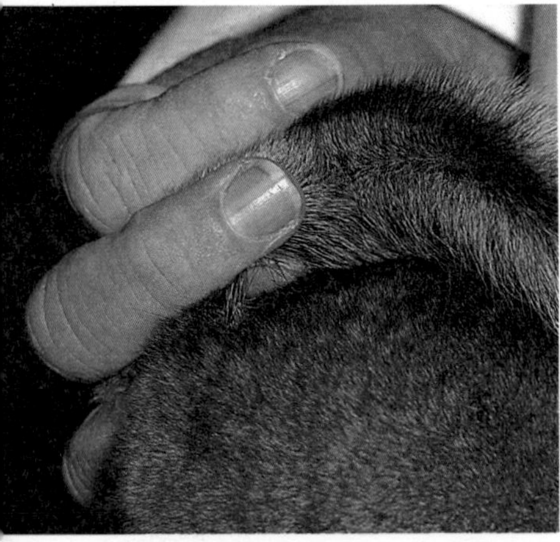

Close-up of the bushy tail of a chinchilla. Never grasp the tail at the tip; it can break off and disfigure an otherwise perfect animal.

Appearance of the plantar surface of the front paw of a chinchilla. Only four digits are fully developed. The thumb is rudimentary.

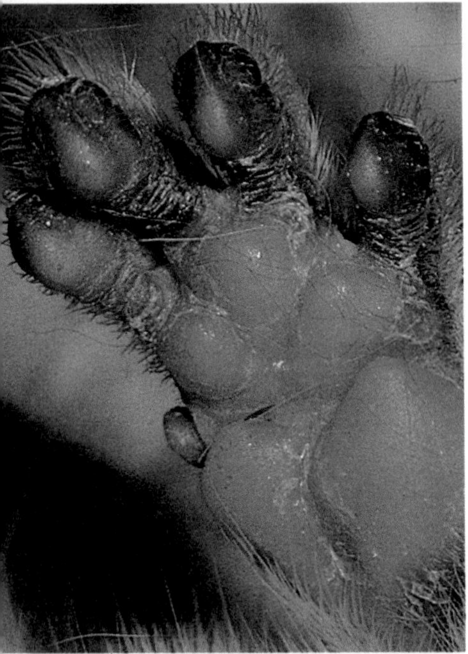

Even though chinchillas have a reputation as gentle animals and good potential pets, careful consideration must be paid to many factors before actually bringing one of them into your home. Your commitment to its care, preparation of its environment, and your own education regarding the pet must all be well considered before any final purchase is made.

PROPER INTRODUCTIONS SHOULD ALWAYS BE CONDUCTED FIRST

While the chinchilla resembles a rabbit with a bushy, squirrel-like tail, they are in fact rodents (rabbits, of course, are not rodents). Most of them have thick, blue-gray fur that is one or more inches in length. Others are seen with brownish gray fur with light blackish tinted markings. Their underparts are yellowish white. They have large eyes and ears and their bushy tails are usually 3 to 10 inches long. The reason their fur is so luxurious is the fact that chinchillas have more fur per square inch than any other known land animal. Fully grown, they measure about 12 inches long and weigh anywhere from 18 to 35 ounces. Most often called does, the females are larger than the bucks or males.

There are some other minor variations, but there are basically two types of chinchillas, both having large hindquarters and small forelimbs with four toes and flexible fingers. The domesticated types are known scientifically as *Chinchilla brevicaudata* and *Chinchilla lanigera.* The "brevicaudata" types have

Facing page: *Standing on its hind feet is not unusual for a chinchilla. However, this behavior is not unique to chinchillas; hamsters, gerbils, mice, and other rodents also stand this way.*

The resemblance of a chinchilla to a "ball of fur" makes it an appealing animal for a pet. It gives one the impression of being a cuddly toy.

thicker necks and shoulders making them appear stockier than the "lanigera" types. They are longer in total length than other types of chinchillas, but their tails are relatively shorter. The "lanigera" type is distinguished by more pointed facial features, a longer tail and narrower neck and shoulders. This makes them appear to be longer and leaner than their brevicaudata brothers, when in fact they are the smaller species. The consensus among mammalogists is that all domesticated chinchillas belong to the species *C. lanigera.*

Chinchillas are considered to be very clean animals and, under normal domesticated circumstances, have no detectable odor. If they are frightened or feel trapped they tend to give off a pungent scorched almond odor. However, this is seldom detected in the variety of chinchillas sold in pet stores. The thickness of their unique fur prevents any odor-causing lice, fleas or other parasites from nesting within.

Chinchillas can make crying and barking noises like many other animals, but seldom make more than a chattering or chirping and a crackling vocalization if angry. They have also been heard making a warning sound like *key-key.*

Being nocturnal animals for the most part, they sleep during the day and are more active from early evening and into the night. In the wild, they have been observed playing in the open during dusk.

They live up to 10 years in the wild and have been reported to have survived up to 20 years in captivity. However, the average lifespan of a pet chinchilla appears to be more on the order of 8 to 10 years.

All of the over 1,000,000 chinchillas now living in the United States call South America their ancestral home. They are indigenous to the snow-covered Andes Mountains, living in the high valleys from Peru and northern Bolivia to southern Chile. They have been found from 3,000 to 15,000 feet up.

While most chinchilla pet owners might not like to think about animals such as theirs becoming part of a coat or other extravagant wrap, the vast majority of American chinchillas face this fate. However, the chinchillas for sale in pet stores were bred as *pets* and were never considered as potential pelts for fur manufacturers.

Perhaps even more disturbing to pet owners is the fact that chinchillas were once included in the diets of the South American Chinca and Inca Indians back in the 1500's when the Spanish explorers first discovered the small animals. These same travelers named the rodents after the Chincas and were responsible for introducing chinchillas to Europe and for almost causing their extinction.

Chinchilla fur became so popular as adornment on the clothes of European royalty that the demand nearly wiped out the chinchilla population. Hunters tracked them and ravaged their natural surroundings. Not only did this result in almost destroying all of the chinchillas, but it also caused them to seek higher and higher territory for safety.

Most of the American chinchillas owe their existence to Mathias F. Chapman. Chapman was a mining engineer who, in 1923, brought 11

In addition to full-length coats, decorative accessories such as the muff shown here, collars, purses and others are manufactured from chinchilla pelts.

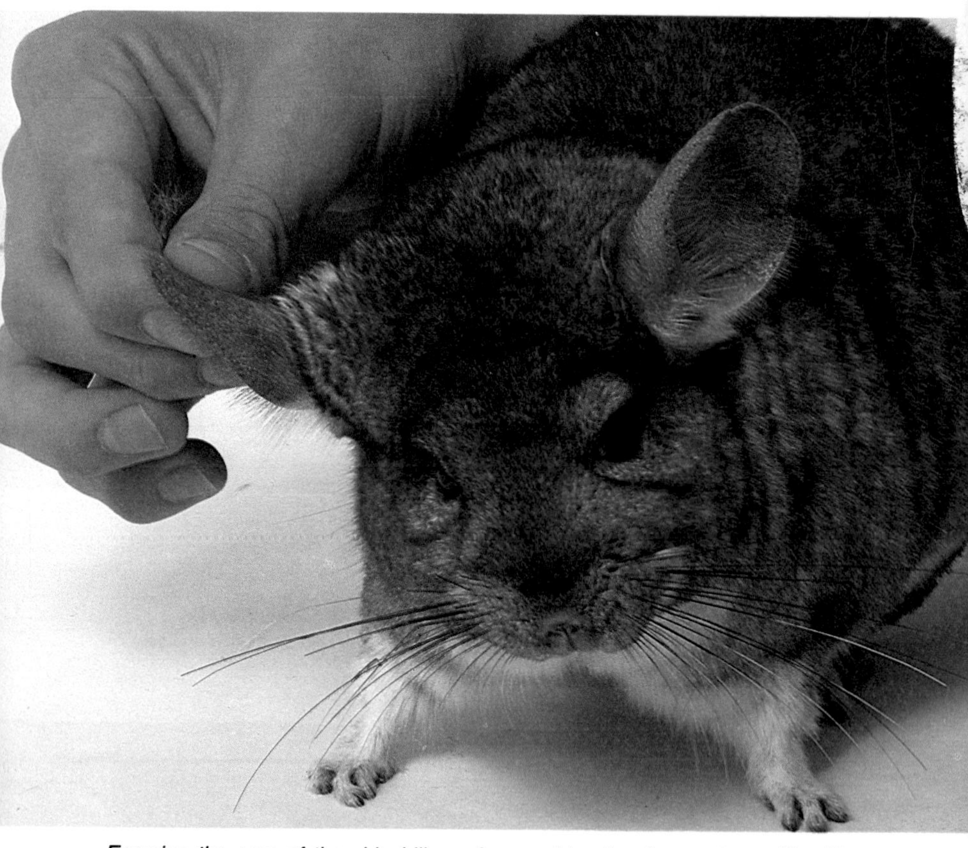

Examine the ears of the chinchilla under consideration for purchase. Handling the ears does not cause pain to a chinchilla, unless an abnormality exists.

chinchillas he'd captured to California. After many experiments with their environment, including different pens and various diets, Chapman achieved success in breeding them. He began selling pairs of the small rodents and, in the short span of four decades, the chinchilla fur industry had spread across the country.

Curiously enough, many of the owners who had established chinchilla fur ranches began considering the desirability of having a chinchilla as a pet, something Chapman had never even considered.

Normally, chinchillas have a gentle nature. However, since they are rodents, they have two incisors at the front of both their upper and lower jaws, no canine teeth, and a number of back cheek teeth. They like to use their incisors to gnaw on things as a form of investigation. Chinchillas have their teeth at birth, and they grow continuously. They constantly require something to chew on. This is one reason why chinchillas cannot have the freedom to roam the house like a pet cat. If allowed to do so, they often head right for the furniture or electrical wiring to sharpen those incisors.

Also, potential chinchilla pet owners should take note that such inquisitive nibbling may be frightening to young handlers. If chinchillas are frightened or cornered they *will* bite. Such a bite can be deep and painful and should be dealt with accordingly.

A chinchilla will not usually use its teeth unless it is picked up in a clumsy manner. If they feel they are being threatened or chased, they depend more on their running and jumping abilities, their lightning-fast agility, and the fact that they are able to shed patches of fur if grabbed. If they manage to escape, they tend to be extremely difficult to recapture.

Many chinchillas will not like to be petted initially unless they are being held firmly. Some pet owners have observed that once the chinchilla becomes used to its handlers, it enjoys being scratched under the chin or behind the ears, much like a cat. In fact, some long-domesticated chinchillas will even beg for more of such attention once put back in their cage. Pets of any kind will become

A dramatic photo illustrating the tendency of a chinchilla to shed fur when frightened. Careful handling is important to avoid unsightly bald spots.

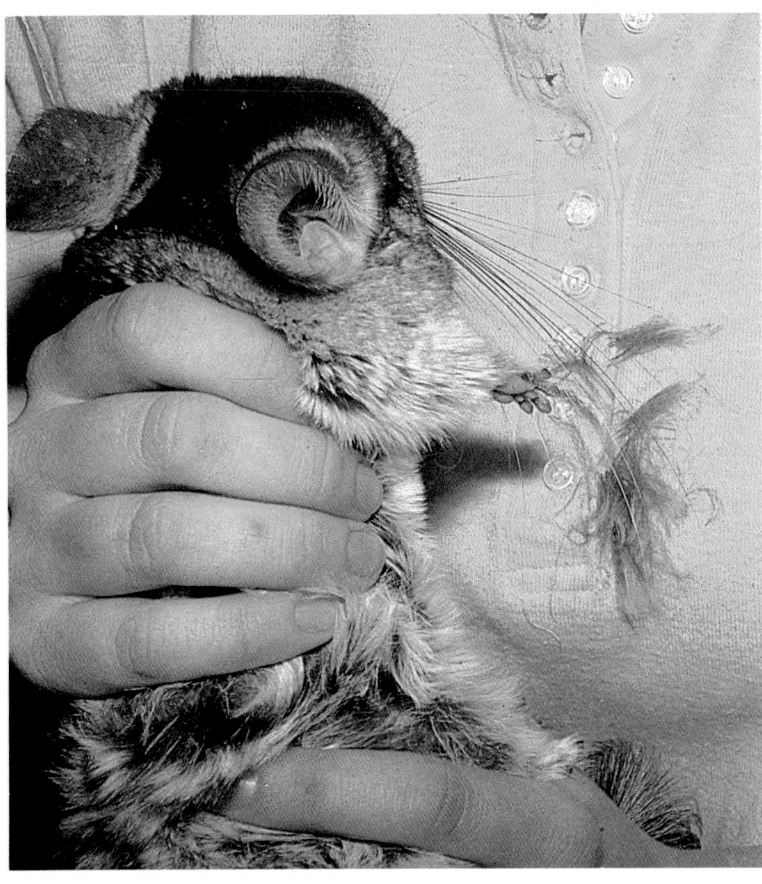

In addition to the common standard gray chinchillas, other color breeds are also available. With increasing demand, pet chinchilla breeders may be inclined to develop mutations that may have been ignored before.

used to some handling and, with more and more generations of chinchillas becoming pets, it is not unlikely that their offspring will become accustomed to handling more readily.

Chinchillas are gregarious among their own kind, but certain other pets in the animal's potential home may pose problems. If there is, for instance, a dog in the house, new chinchilla owners must be prepared to keep the canine away from the rodents or supervise them until it's certain the dog won't do any harm to the chinchilla.

Curiously, cats are less dangerous to chinchillas than dogs, but similar precautions should be taken if a cat already lives in the chinchilla's future home. Also, if your chinchilla is to be part of a collection of rare and unusual pets, remember that snakes and ferrets are a chinchilla's natural enemies. They must be kept apart at all times.

Chinchillas are strict vegetarians, making feeding relatively easy and inexpensive. Since the popularity of chinchilla ranching grew in the late 50's, advanced chinchilla pellets are available in most good pet stores and are the dietary staple of the animals. While it is advisable to keep chinchillas on a regular feeding schedule, if adequate amounts of chinchilla pellets and water are easily accessible they can be left unattended in their cage for a couple of days. They do not require daily outings.

Similar to other young pets such as puppies and kittens, young chinchillas are intelligent, inquisitive animals with a natural ability to devise their own amusing pasttimes. Children and adults find them fun to play with and a delight to watch. Even the older pet chinchillas never appear to grow out of this stage, enjoying active play long into what is considered "old age" for a rodent.

Any small animal which is being considered as a pet should grow used to handling in a short period of time and should not frantically struggle to get free when picked up. The only time such a reaction might be expected is if the animal has become frightened. Loud noises and sudden movements tend to terrify chinchillas. Most notable are "hissing" or "swishing" noises and movements which cause shadows to fall within the chinchilla's sight. The prevailing theory is that such sounds and movements make the chinchillas believe that snakes, one of their natural enemies, are nearby. It is important to avoid any actions which will produce the aforementioned results when first approaching a chinchilla since it will make it hard to catch and handle a potential pet. It will also make it difficult to determine the actual personality of the individual chinchilla. When selecting one for a pet, personality is one of the most important factors to consider.

Other factors include such things as age or sex. Most baby chinchillas are weaned after approximately eight weeks of age. Experts feel that these chinchillas should not leave their mothers for at least a couple of weeks after that. Most often, people prefer buying a young animal between three and four months of age, enabling them to watch its growth and to enjoy seeing it discover its world.

View of a display table in a chinchilla show. Chinchilla shows are generally open to the public and can be an opportunity for viewing the best animals around.

A standard gray chinchilla mother and her young. It is definitely not recommended to purchase unweaned chinchillas.

Since there is no evidence that male chinchillas are more gentle or more attractive than females, there is little concern over the sex of the potential pet. Most pet owners begin with a single animal, others start out with a pair. This latter group has to be prepared to care for offspring. Unless the pair were already cohabiting before they were bought, it is wise to introduce them gradually. It is possible to cage more than two together, but this should only be a grouping of one buck and several does. Two females or two males should never be caged together.

Approaching any new venture requires preparation. Now that we've examined the history and characteristics of this potential pet, it is time to examine exactly how to prepare for your chinchilla to move in with you.

Three color mutations of chinchillas bred on a chinchilla ranch. These are prime specimens and not available to the general public.

Selection and Handling

Selection of your pet chinchilla is a very important task. The best place to begin searching is your local telephone book. You can look for good pet stores, or there might be a chinchilla ranch in your area which sells some of their stock as pets. If no pet stock is available, it is a good bet that one or more of these contacts will be able to suggest somewhere else to search. As with any purchase, thorough pre-shopping will determine the best price. The prices will probably vary, but keep in mind that you are shopping for a pet, not a champion chinchilla. As long as it is a healthy, happy, gentle animal, you've probably chosen well.

As we mentioned earlier, many people choose such a pet as a companion for a youngster. While surprising a child on a holiday or birthday is exciting and fun, a "surprise pet" (of any kind) is not a good suggestion. A child must be prepared to take care of a pet properly. This includes knowing how to feed, touch and otherwise oversee its well-being. In shopping for a pet, it is wise to bring the potential child owner along. Save other gifts for "surprises."

Remember that along with the chinchilla a cage, food and other accessories must be considered in the initial purchase cost. These items will be discussed a little further on. For now, let's assume that you have found a pet store that deals in chinchillas and you've come in for your first look.

Some stores do not display their chinchillas for various reasons. Since

Chinchillas are sensitive animals and respond to soft sounds you utter. Loud noises make them nervous and apprehensive.

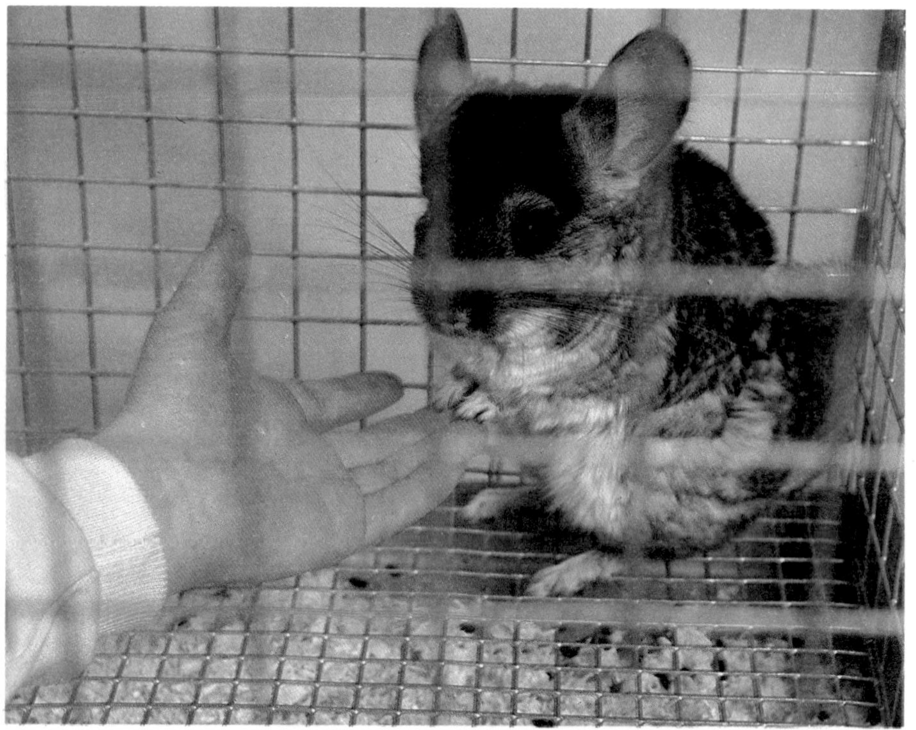

When approached by a stranger, a chinchilla's first reaction is to withdraw into a corner of the cage. This reaction disappears when it no longer feels threatened.

they are nocturnal animals, they are not very active during the day like a small puppy or kitten. Also, their natural fear of movement and noise makes it desirable for them not to be frequently displayed as a general rule. Calling for an appointment to view them is often required. This depends, of course, on the policy of your local pet store.

As with any small pet, it is a good practice to closely examine it before buying. One of the major factors to keep in mind is proper handling of the animal. The way you initially touch and hold a chinchilla will not determine if the one you have is the one you want, but it can help you decide if having a chinchilla in the first place is a good idea for you. Pet shop owners will allow handling of the animal under their supervision. They are the experts in caring for these animals and can answer your questions about the history and supervision of the animal. They will appreciate it if your examination of your potential pet is an educated one, enabling you to ask the right questions about maintaining its health.

When holding a chinchilla, there are important guidelines to remember. First of all, be sure you approach the chinchilla quietly and gently. It is even a good idea to speak softly to the animal, letting it become used to the sound of your voice. As we mentioned, loud noises and quick movements tend to terrify them. Potential handlers should

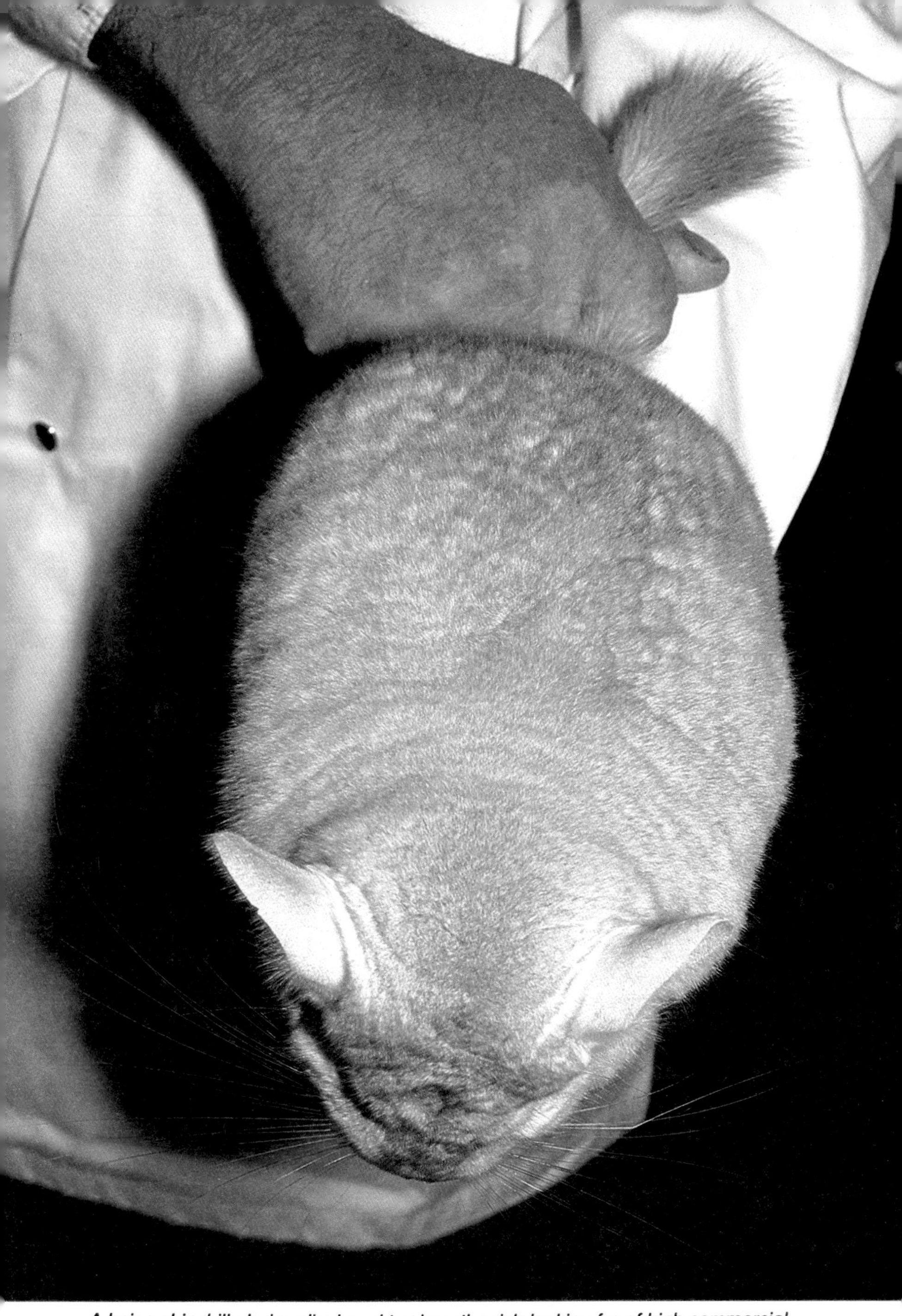

A beige chinchilla being displayed to show the rich-looking fur of high commercial value. This specimen is correctly handled, although the hand supporting the abdomen is not visible.

allow the chinchilla to "get to know" their hands by actually reaching into the chinchilla's cage. The chinchilla's incisors are a major tool in its examining new objects. As long as you reach into the cage with great care, there is little danger in getting bitten. They will not bite hard unless they feel unduly threatened. They will most likely nibble on sleeves or rings or other bright jewelry rather than the hand. As an illustration of how gentle this investigative chewing really is, chinchillas are often observed nibbling around each other's faces and ears as a form of affection.

Since the chinchilla is able to shed patches of skin if grabbed by its fur, this should never be attempted. When the animal appears used to the handler's hand, then it can be lifted. The best way to do this is when the animal is facing you. Reach around and secure a firm grasp on its tail with one hand and support its body with the other. Chinchilla breeders can often be seen lifting the animal by pinching its ears together and holding it or by grabbing it by its tail. In both of these cases, they immediately support the animal's body from underneath. They never leave it dangling. This can be dangerous to the chinchilla, especially when handling a pregnant female. If you do pick it up by its tail initially remember to hold it at the point closest to its body to prevent the possible breaking off of the tip. Perhaps the best rule is to never pick up a chinchilla by its tail.

Holding and lifting the chinchilla is not only to see if you and the animal are compatible, but you should use this opportunity to determine the appearance and general health of the animal. One determines the other.

First, get the "feel" of the animal in your hand. It should be "solid" and weigh about one to two pounds when fully grown. Chinchillas are considered fully grown at approximately eight months of age; however, they are usually weaned after only ten or eleven weeks. They are able to leave their mothers at this time and many shoppers prefer a younger animal as a pet. This allows the joy of watching them growing and exploring their surroundings. Of course, the younger the animal, the more years it will have as a pet. The disadvantages of having a younger chinchilla include the facts that they may not be as used to handling at a younger age and that some chinchillas do not take well to separation from their mothers. Some that have been weaned too early have experienced sickness and even death. Studies have indicated that the period of time right after a young chinchilla weans up to when it reaches about three months of age is when most deaths take place among the younger animals. Sadly, this is often due to new owners feeding the smaller chinchillas as if they could handle an adult diet. We will be covering proper feeding of chinchillas later on. We note this at this point only to illustrate a possible advantage for a new owner in purchasing a full-grown animal for a pet.

Facing page: *Top, young chinchillas can be carried on the palm of the hand. Allow them to approach and climb of their own volition. Left, for lifting correctly, the ears are pinched together, the tail is held close to the base, then the hand holding the ears is moved quickly to support the belly. Right, never dangle the animal by the tail, which can break off or have the entire skin sloughed off, leaving a naked tail.*

A chinchilla's eyes should be free of sores and unsightly crusts. They should reflect an alert disposition, not a lethargic or morose look.

Eyes and teeth should be examined next. You should look straight into the eyes, making certain they appear clear and bright. Clear and bright eyes are an indication of good health. If the eyes are teary, it is probably an indication of an existing health problem or one which is about to show itself. One such cause of watery eyes might be dental problems in the animal.

The eyes are relatively easy to check, but you might prefer the help of an expert in observing the chinchilla's teeth. It is essential to make a careful examination of the chinchilla's mouth. Like many small animals, it will most likely be reluctant to have its mouth forced open to provide a clear view. Also, rodents have very narrow mouth openings, making such examinations difficult. However, your pet shop owner or chinchilla rancher will probably be able to handle the animal so you can get a quick look. A good way to do it on your own is to, if the owner will allow it, offer the chinchilla an acceptable treat of some kind or let it chew harmlessly on some object. While it is doing this, you will be able to view its front teeth, which, oddly enough, should be yellow or orange-yellow in color instead of white.

Being rodents, chinchillas' incisors grow continuously. Their normal chewing and gnawing actions naturally grind down the teeth. Chinchillas that have been well cared for are usually provided such things as pumice stones or hardwood branches from fruit trees for this gnawing exercise. If all is well, the tips of the top pair of teeth should be straight across.

Healthy chinchillas should eat rapidly and, when eating, the animal should not drool or appear to be pawing around the area of its mouth. If it does drool, or if it has wet or matted hair on its chin that indicates it *has* been drooling, there could very well be a problem with the animal's teeth. Problems with the teeth pose serious difficulties for the animal from simple eating to good digestion. If there is any indication of such problems in an animal you're examining, point it out to the seller and look for a different chinchilla as a potential pet.

If you have made an appointment to view a chinchilla, it is likely that the pet shop owner or chinchilla rancher has cleaned the cage prior to your visit. Even if this is the case, ask to view the animal's droppings. Chinchilla droppings are one of the best ways of judging the overall health of the animals.

There are no completely "normal droppings" since the varieties of food and liquid given to the animals play a very important part in the consistency and color of any feces. Veterinarians and chinchilla ranchers who have studied the many different chinchilla stocks often report that animals with "abnormal" droppings can still enjoy a long life.

As should be expected, each chinchilla is an individual animal, and its droppings will have their own

Well formed chinchilla teeth are even, straight, free of jagged edges, and yellow in color.

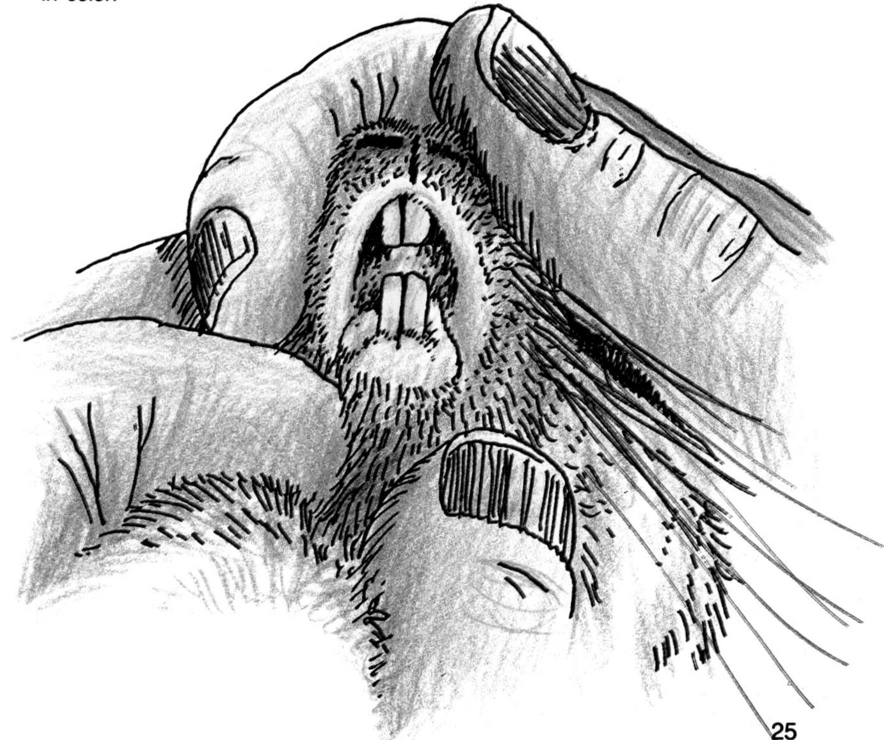

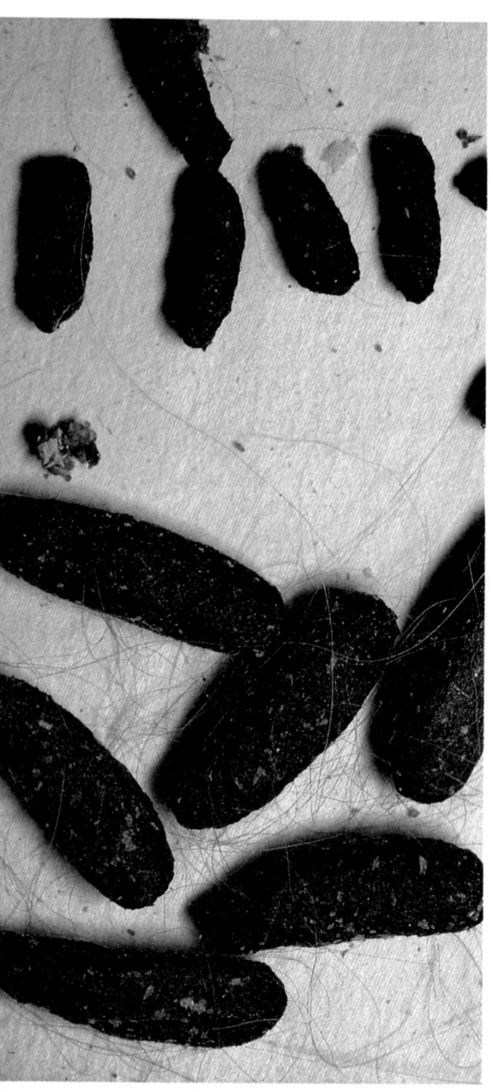

Droppings are indicators of your chinchilla's health. Those below are normal droppings from a healthy chinchilla. The small ones above came from a constipated animal.

specific characteristics. However, there are some important normalities and abnormalities that should be taken into consideration. Chinchilla feces should be almost dry and a brownish greenish in color. Healthy chinchillas should produce feces which are uniform in size, elongated, plump, oval or rounded, firm and slightly moist. After breaking the droppings apart, they should not have any hollow cavities where undigested food remains are found. If feces have drawn-out, pointed ends and a slimy coating, it is almost always a sign of digestive disorder.

Although somewhat disturbing to a novice chinchilla owner, it is not out of the ordinary for a chinchilla to eat part of its droppings to maintain a proper bacterial content in its system.

As pointed out earlier, there is no particular advantage in selecting a male or female chinchilla as a pet. Studies and reports from chinchilla breeders and owners indicate no difference in the general appearance or attitudes of either sex. As a pet, health and your own compatibility with a specific animal are the factors to take into consideration. Since the pet chinchillas are not "breeding stock" *per se,* they all tend to be of the silver-gray or "standard" variety. Others that you may come across are beige, white and black. Additionally, there may be small, individual characteristic markings, but since you are not looking for fur production, this should be of little or no concern beyond an esthetic judgment.

When first viewing chinchillas you might also observe their dust baths. Although some breeders have been known to shampoo their stock, chinchillas dislike being wet. They bathe not in water but in a finely ground powder. They appear to prefer a dust similar to the volcanic ash found in the Andes, which is the kind their ancestors probably utilized. Normally, the dust bath is enjoyed by the animals during the early morning hours. Since, as we've noted previously, they are more active during the hours of darkness, they take their dust baths after periods of high activity. Opinions differ on the specific hygienic requirements of the chinchilla dust bath, but it does serve to clean, massage and otherwise care for the animal's pelts by removing excess natural oils.

If it is your desire to own a pair of chinchillas as pets there are additional considerations. First and foremost is that the pair must be of opposite sexes. Two buck chinchillas or two doe chinchillas caged together are not compatible. Secondly, it is best that you purchase a pair that have already been living in the same cage. If they have been cohabiting in the pet store, they have had the opportunity to get used to one another. If you do buy separate chinchillas and want to have them share a cage, they must be introduced gradually. If this is the case, it might be necessary to buy separate quarters for each one for a time. This will, naturally, add to your initial cost.

Housing a pair of chinchillas increases the chance of offspring. We'll be discussing the care of baby chinchillas somewhat later on. We mention it here to remind the first-time chinchilla owner of the possible added commitment that must be made for owning a pair. The advantages of starting out with a single animal seem to out-weigh the possible desire to begin with a pair.

Beyond these precautions, it might be wise, if possible, to find a chinchilla pet owner. Their advice and insights on the problems and joys they have faced will make a world of difference in selecting your own pet. It might be a good idea to observe their pet during the day, while it is feeding, playing and sleeping. This would undoubtedly influence your own decision on whether or not owning a chinchilla is the right move for you.

Pet shop owners, chinchilla ranchers and veterinarians are still your best source of useful and expert advice. Even if the shop owners or ranchers do not have any chinchillas for sale or in stock, they will help you prepare for when the pets finally move into your home.

A necessary piece of equipment in a chinchilla's cage is a receptacle for taking a dust bath. Watching a chinchilla dusting itself is quite fascinating.

Your Chinchilla's Home

Your chinchilla should be kept in a simple wire cage. However, there are some exacting specifications for chinchilla cages which are the result of years of observation and study on the part of chinchilla owners, ranchers and breeders.

When Mathias F. Chapman first herded his 11 chinchillas, he noted that they lived in deep crevices between boulders. In his efforts to both duplicate these surroundings and to be able to observe his herd in their new California home, he constructed unique burrows surrounded by large pens made from wire. He then made small houses of concrete resembling ovens and partially buried them in the ground. Openings were in each house to let the animals in and out and to give Chapman access. He hoped these would provide dark, quiet, cool places for the animals which would most closely duplicate their South American homes.

However, Chapman soon found that such burrows were impractical and he tried simple wire cages. Wire cages similar to Chapman's have since become the standard pet and breeding chinchilla residences.

Each adult chinchilla should have its own cage. Even though the animals are known to normally have a gentle disposition, they do not get along well with their own kind in close quarters. A cage for a single adult should measure approximately 18 to 24 inches deep, 16 to 24 inches wide and 12 to 22 inches high. It should be constructed from easy-to-clean materials. Cages with galvanized point-welded wire mesh are one of the most popular types since they are rustproof and easy to keep sanitary. While they are advertised as being easy to clean, cages with plastic coated wire should be avoided. Always remember that your chinchilla is a chewer and a nibbler. Such plastic coating is an easy chewing target. The plastic is probably non-toxic, but chewed plastic shreds can make a royal mess of your cage. Additionally, cages constructed from wood or ordinary chicken wire are not recommended.

The size of the mesh on your cage should be an important consideration. Naturally, it should be small enough to keep your chinchilla in. However, if you are planning on keeping a pair, remember that baby chinchillas might be able to escape through a mesh that would be too small for the parents to squeeze through. A mother chinchilla's cage must not have mesh openings one inch square or larger or the babies will be able to wriggle out.

While you should get direct advice from your pet shop owner, there are two varieties of wire cages used by most chinchilla breeders and owners. Each has different advantages. As long as you remember to keep them away from drafts (which may be too cool for your chinchilla), wire-bottom cages do a great deal in helping keep the animal very clean. These cages allow the chinchilla droppings, loose feed and other small chewing debris to fall through. Newspapers are usually positioned on a drop pan beneath the cage. These drop pans are made of metal or a piece of plastic and they serve to catch the waste, making disposal and cleaning easy. A metal drop pan will be easier to keep clean if it has a couple of coats of

Facing page: *An array of cages at a commercial chinchilla farm. Each compartment is not visually isolated from the adjoining unit. Hay troughs serve adjoining compartments. A food hopper and a resting platform are in each unit. Water is delivered by an automatic watering system, not by water bottles in this setup.*

rust-proof paint on it. Since you can use every-day newspapers instead of litter as in solid-bottom cages, supplies for wire-bottom cages are very inexpensive. Remember, however, that the newspaper covering under wire-bottom cages needs to be changed daily.

Cages with solid bottoms are the most popular among pet owners simply because they are easier to maintain. It also appears that this type of cage is more comfortable for the chinchilla. Most of these cages come with a pull-out drawer for easy cleaning and filling like those found on most bird cages.

The sides and the top of the cage should be kept clean. A moist or damp rag should do the trick with some aid of a brush to pick up hair, food or other debris which may have become lodged in the mesh.

The bottom of the chinchilla's cage should be covered by two to three inches of litter consisting of materials such as wood shavings or other absorbent substances. Various products have been tried and tested for filling chinchilla cage bottoms. At first, you might assume that some cat litters could be used for chinchillas. If they are manufactured from ground clay and they have not been treated with odor neutralizers or other chemicals, they might be suitable. However, any substitute which has not been thoroughly tested under exacting experimentation by experts could cause some difficulties and dangers.

Sawdust has been used with success by some breeders if it is changed often. Others complain that

This cage has a solid bottom constructed of galvanized iron. It can be pulled out for replacement of the bedding and droppings.

A type of cage with wire walls and floor. The cardboard box provides a place for retreat during daylight hours, when a chinchilla generally sleeps.

sawdust is too easily thrown out of the cage by the normal activity of the chinchilla. This not only means an empty cage bottom for the chinchilla, but also a terrible mess to clean up around its cage. Corn cobs ground to a mulch are also very absorbent and they are inexpensive. However, like sawdust, they can easily be thrown out of the cage. Corn cobs are often known to carry mites. These probably won't bother the chinchilla, but no one wants mites in their home.

Sand is very absorbent but usually unsuitable. It absorbs moisture naturally from the air and retains it. In turn, the chinchilla's fur absorbs this moisture from the sand, causing the animal to appear messy. This state is probably uncomfortable for the animal as well. Hay and straw can be used, but for very short periods of time. Mold will set in if they are not changed frequently and this can discolor the animal's fur.

Specially treated and scented wood shavings specifically manufactured for use in the bottoms of chinchilla cages are now relatively inexpensive and easy to find. Most quality pet stores carry them even if they don't stock chinchillas. Wood shavings provide a comfortable bedding for the animals.

As we continually note, chinchillas love to chew. Be careful in selecting the type of wood shavings you use. Avoid those which have been chemically treated. Some such shavings could have come from wood which has been lacquered,

glued, stained or painted. All such wood poses a serious threat to the health of your pet. There have been some sad reports in the past telling of such shavings leading to fatal poisoning of prized chinchillas.

A number of professional chinchilla breeders strongly advise keeping away from using any kind of cedar wood shavings as well. There is a theory that the resin in cedar shavings may be harmful to the animals. Their preferences are softwood shavings like those from pinewood. It is best to use those recommended by your local pet shop owner.

Many chinchilla owners and experts advise the use of fuller's earth as a litter. It is a soft, absorbent material resembling clay, commonly used in removing grease from areas about to be filled. It is white and pebbly in appearance and available in different weights and sizes, depending on the screening process used. If it is mixed occasionally, it can also be left in place up to a month at a time. The coarse mix is better for use with chinchillas since the finer variety is much too absorbent, taking and retaining excessive moisture. This finer variety also tends to stick to the animals' fur when moist.

Fuller's earth is a specialty product and is not as commonly used as wood shavings. If you want to use it, ask your pet shop owner if he has some in stock or if he can special-order it for you. Fuller's earth

Any small animal litter, except cedar wood, is acceptable for lining the bottom of a cage.

may present a dry skin problem in your pet simply because it *is* so absorbent. If you observe your animal scratching too much, this may be a sign of dry skin caused by the fuller's earth. If you suspect this is a problem, switch to wood shavings.

The overall guideline to remember is that any experimentation on your part regarding the immediate environment of your pet chinchilla might endanger its life. It's best to follow the recommendations of your pet shop owner or stay with tried and true materials.

Along with your chinchilla's cage, you will have to purchase a number of accessory items for your pet's food, water and recreation. The main staple of a chinchilla's diet is chinchilla pellets. However, they also enjoy a variety of grains and hay. We shall be detailing proper diet later on. We make mention of it here with our housing specifications since you must provide the proper food and water containers in your chinchilla's cage. If you plan to feed your

A heavy ceramic bowl and a water bottle are basic necessities for keeping a chinchilla. Situated outside, this plastic water bottle is out of reach of your gnawing chinchilla. However, the spout must be of strong material, glass or metal, which can withstand chewing.

chinchilla any kind of supplement or hay, more containers than the ones we'll mention below will be needed.

There are a number of small containers designed specifically for chinchilla pellets. One of the most popular is the variety which can be attached to the side of the cage. However, many owners use elevated, shallow glass or porcelain bowls which have been glazed on the inside. These coaster-like containers are easy for the chinchillas to use, but they must be weighted so that they will not be tipped over by the animal's constant moving. Also, the elevation prevents most of the pellets from being scattered and litter from being kicked into it as the chinchilla scurries around. Placing

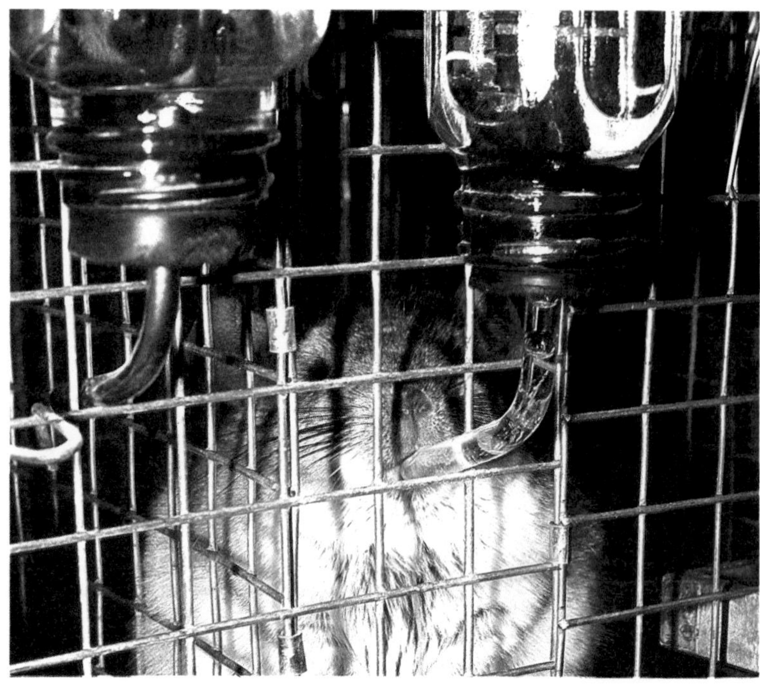

A chinchilla savoring fresh clean water. Clean water is crucial to the survival of small animals. Bacteria and mold grow in stale water and cause a number of diseases, some of which are fatal.

the bowl slightly higher than the floor prevents the animal from sitting on it or getting food soiled with their droppings or urine.

One of the most common uses for the coaster dishes is for a special treat or supplements. The dishes can be quickly removed from the cage since a chinchilla will normally complete such treats in a single sitting. Since many chinchilla owners feel it is wise to avoid constantly opening and closing the cage for each bathing, feeding and watering operation, these special food bowls are often slid into the cages directly through a small opening in the wire mesh designed specifically for that purpose. Also, a movable wire is attached to the bowl which can prevent it from being pushed around by the animal.

Chinchillas are able to drink from such coasters, but even a small amount of litter or pellets will contaminate or pollute their water. The best policy is to obtain a water system which is closed from the chinchillas except for drinking. A small metal- or glass-tubed bottle attached on the side of the cage is usually the kind used. Avoid plastic-tubed bottles since they will be chewed up by the animal in a very short time. Also, if you choose a plastic bottle for your water system (with a glass or metal tube), remember to position it in such a manner as to prevent the animal from chewing on the bottle itself. Check the water bottle daily and always be certain your pet is supplied with ample drinking water. Whichever kind of bottle you use, it must be cleaned daily, with the animals receiving a fresh supply of water with every feeding. Water that they didn't drink with their previous feeding should be discarded. Before re-filling the bottles, they should be thoroughly rinsed. A complete cleaning with mild dish washing detergent and a complete rinsing with clean water should be done about twice a week. When doing this, be certain that any algal growth has been removed from the bottle, stopper and tube. Algal growth is dangerous to the chinchilla's health and could lead to illness or death. Food dishes should also be cleaned on a regular basis since any uneaten portion is subject to dangerous contamination.

If you are keeping a pair (or more) of chinchillas, those that become ill must be separated from the others. All professional chinchilla ranchers have a quarantine cage. Such separate cages should have a whole separate set of cleaning tools.

If you are replacing an animal which has died and are using the same cage, it should be thoroughly disinfected before your new chinchilla moves in. Common household disinfectants are adequate for cleanings, but "burning out" all-metal cages with a blow torch is one way to be completely certain that even the most resistant germs will be destroyed.

If you have one or more chinchillas, new animals which are

Any situation that brings about dampness in a chinchilla's environment must be avoided. Placing plants on top of or close to the cage is not recommended.

In general, hay sold by a reputable pet shop is clean and well processed. Alfalfa is considered a very good hay and marketed as loose hay or in cubes.

purchased should be isolated from the others for the first few weeks as a precaution against possible contagious diseases or any lack of immunities which may be present.

Hay for chinchillas is available both as cubes and loose. Holders for both varieties are currently available. However, there have been some complaints that certain hay holders do not secure the food well enough to compensate for the animal's eating motion. In a very short time, the food has slid out of the chinchilla's reach. Be certain that the hay is held securely. These holders come in a style which can be attached to the wall, placed on the floor, or both. In the case of loose hay, it is usually best to have it hang well above the floor, near the door.

Harking back to their mountain origins, chinchillas thrive the best in moderate temperatures below 80 degrees Fahrenheit. Above that, they become very uncomfortable. In temperatures of 90 degrees Fahrenheit they are in danger of dying. This is one of the reasons you should take extreme caution in selecting the location of your pet's cage. The location of your cage should be considered part of your pet's ongoing hygiene. Make certain that your chinchilla's cage stays out of rooms which tend to be damp or drafty. If the room you've chosen tends to become warm during the day, try to see that the air can be kept in motion as long as it does not create a draft directly on the animal. Avoid placing the cage in direct sunlight or in uninsulated rooms such as basements, attics or garages. Don't keep it outside; it could be subjected to extreme temperatures, and its inhabitants could escape and never be seen again.

If your pet's room is an active thoroughfare during the day, it's a good suggestion to provide the cage with a covering similar to those used for birds. Your chinchilla's cover would give the animal the isolation it needs while it is resting. Its resting time will usually be during the daytime, but they normally become used to disturbances. The covering will make it easier for them to adjust.

Since chinchillas are very, very active during the night, they obviously need certain things in their cages which will help them expend some of their excess energy. Most importantly, they constantly need something to chew on. This is

A chinchilla starting to nibble hay from a newly placed supply. The strange collar on this female is a device that inhibits it from going through an opening in its cage that permits a smaller male to pass through.

A few items, usually found in the home, usable as chew toys for your chinchilla. However, be sure that any products you choose are non-poisonous.

without regard to the animal's age. Even older chinchillas need to satisfy their chewing urge to keep their teeth sharp and in condition. Wood or pumice blocks can be purchased at your pet store. In fact, your pet store owner will probably recommend such a purchase when you buy your chinchilla. The animals will not only chew on these items, but will use them as toys, rolling them around and picking them up. Watching this kind of play is the major source of the delight in owning a chinchilla.

Any kind of wooden block can be used. Avoid wood which has been lacquered, glued, stained or painted, and stay away from cedar. Pumice is merely spongy volcanic lava usually used as an abrasive and polishing material. It can be purchased as ready-to-use chew block squares or in larger pieces. The bigger pieces can then be sawed into smaller four-inch square shapes which will probably last a long time.

Other items you might want to include are juice cans with the top and bottom removed so the chinchilla can use them as a place to hide or sleep in, exercise wheels, cardboard tubes, etcetera. You might also consider having a small carpet remnant square in the cage for your chinchilla. They will sleep on it, chew it and otherwise play with it. Your chinchilla will also appreciate having some thick branches for jumping, climbing and, of course, chewing.

Although chinchillas' natural habitat is the cool climate of the Andes, they have often been observed basking in the late afternoon and morning sunlight. They will almost always seek the warmest area when they're ready to sleep. For extra pampering of some pet chinchillas, owners have installed a heating pad. If the pad is flat, hard, uses low wattage and is positioned so the animal cannot reach it or chew on the cord, it can be an extra comfort for them. Such pads can be slid under a solid bottom cage or spring-held beneath a wire bottom cage. If you don't want to use a heating pad, heat lamps over a corner of the cage can be used instead. They do not have to be in constant operation either. It's best to have them on if the room is drafty or cool or when the animal is asleep or ill.

Since water is scarce in the high Andes, chinchillas have evolved into animals who dislike damp conditions. Nevertheless, they do like to bathe and provisions must be made for frequent baths. However, we're talking about a *dust* bath.

A chinchilla's dust bath serves to clean their thick coats. As they turn, flip over and rub themselves in the dust it rushes through their fur and removes excess natural oils and moisture. It also helps to loosen the fur again. To avoid the transmission of infectious diseases or parasites, each animal should have its own dust bath. Most breeders feel that dust baths must be offered to the animals on a daily basis, preferably before their morning meal. Since chinchillas tend to be typical nocturnal animals, the majority of their active playing, fighting, mating and other activities take place at night; their skin respiration is inhibited and their fur is matted in the morning. Pet owners generally feel that a dust bath twice a week is adequate. They agree that if the animal's fur feels damp to the touch, appears to lie down or separate as the chinchilla moves, then the animal needs to be bathed more often. They have also expressed the opinion that a daily dust bath during especially humid weather may be necessary.

It has been observed that chinchillas that have not had a dust bath for a long period of time get used to not having one. Once the habit of not bathing has set in, the chinchilla can not be persuaded to use their dust bath again. Additionally, if a young chinchilla has not been introduced to a dust bath while nursing, it will not use one after it is weaned. It is important to learn from your pet shop owner whether or not your potential pet chinchilla is a dust bather and to understand the difference.

Chinchilla breeders and pet owners utilize various kinds of dust or sand bath tubs. Only very fine sands and dusts are suitable and it is up to each individual to determine which is best for his chinchilla. Special chinchilla dust is available in many quality pet shops, and pet shop owners will be able to recommend what they feel is best. Some brands of chinchilla bath are available only in

Experience will indicate to you the type of dust bath material that will be most beneficial to your chinchilla. Chinchilla specialists are not agreed on the frequency, but all agree that chinchillas need such baths.

bulk, but buying it in such large quantities should not be a problem since it is inexpensive and can be made to last indefinitely. If specific chinchilla bath is not available, most pet shop owners will suggest a finely ground powder, a dust similar to volcanic ash found in the Andes. In nature, chinchillas bathe in this powdered volcanic ash. Pumice or Fuller's earth has also been used with success. Fine-grained clean quartz sand can be used, but if it is, talcum powder should be added. Coarse quartz sand, brick layer's sand, river sand, or sand from open sand pits should be completely avoided. Naturally, the dust bath becomes slightly soiled with urine each time the chinchilla uses it. In order for this not to stain the animal's fur, the dust must be stirred. Droppings can be removed by sifting the dust. Frequent cleaning of recommended dusts prevents having to continually replace them. If this is done, you only have to replace the top layer on occasion.

An ordinary cat litter box serves well as a container for the dust bath material. It is convenient to use, and easy to clean and store.

There are a wide variety of receptacles which are excellent for a chinchilla dust bath. A rectangular bread pan-size pan, a cat litter pan, a cut turpentine can with the rough edges bent down, and a large glass jar on its side all make practical dust baths. They all keep the dust confined and prevent wholesale scattering. These containers should, at the same time, be small enough to fit through the opening of your pet's cage.

Prescribing to the theories of both a daily dust bath and that frequent opening and closing of the cage is not a good idea, you may wish to make the dust bath container a permanent part of your pet's enclosure. However, since a dust bath should not exceed 10 to 15 minutes for each animal, you should rig a resting board or perch over the dust bath so it can be opened and closed from outside the cage. The edges of the perch should be made of or reinforced by metal strips so they won't be chewed apart. Also, if you are raising additional pets, be certain the top closes securely so that baby chinchillas won't be trapped or strangled by the dust bath lid.

Additional accessories and special comforts for your chinchilla can be recommended by your pet shop owner. Since they have observed the animal for a time before your purchase, they may have specific advice regarding your pet's individual needs and idiosyncrasies.

Now that you've chosen your pet and purchased all it needs for proper housing, recreation, watering and feeding, it is time to determine exactly what these amusing little rodents eat.

What to Feed Your Chinchilla

As we have mentioned previously, chinchilla pellets are readily available in any good pet store. There are several types of commercial chinchilla pellets and they are mostly made up from the same ingredients, a combination of vitamins, minerals, soybean oil, alfalfa meal, wheat germ, molasses, oats and corn. This blend has proven to be of high nutritional value for chinchillas.

However, many brands cater to the chinchilla breeders and ranchers rather than to the pet owners. These brands are available only in 50-pound bags. After such bags are opened, they tend to lose a great deal of their nutritional value after a couple of months. Since a single chinchilla or a pair would never work their way through 50 pounds of pellets in that amount of time, buying a large bag would probably do more harm than good in the long run.

A careful search of your local pet stores will usually net a good source of chinchilla pellets for your pet or pets. If you have difficulty in obtaining an economical supply of specific chinchilla food, there are some viable alternatives.

Many pet owners have opted for rabbit pellets, which are cheaper and are sold in smaller packages as a general rule. These work well for a time. Many have discovered that, because rabbit pellets are fortified with hormones, rabbit pellet-fed chinchillas tend to become fat after a six-month diet. The animals become lazy and their general well-being is often not best served with rabbit pellets.

Some brands of guinea pig pellets contain similar ingredients and can be used in place of other varieties of pellets. This kind of feed is more widely acceptable than rabbit

A chinchilla starting to eat the pelleted food ration offered on the chinchilla farm. Specially formulated chinchilla foods are available at pet shops.

The increasing popularity of chinchillas has resulted in the availability of small packages of pelleted foods designed specifically for chinchillas, reducing chinchilla fanciers' reliance on foods designed for guinea pigs and rabbits.

pellets specifically because of its higher nutritional content and the simple fact that it has a *lower* fat content. As a pet owner, one of these two choices is probably best.

Since your pet has been in the care of the pet shop owner for a time, it is important that you continue the same diet the animal has been on for the first few weeks that it is in your care. If your pet has clear eyes, is active and appears to be in good health, you should feel comfortable about continuing its pet store diet. If you have to change the diet for any reason, it must be done slowly. You can do this by adding small amounts of the new feed within the old supply, slightly increasing its content until it completely replaces the old brand. Being creatures of habit, your chinchilla might at first detect the new feed and ignore it. However, in a short time it will become used to seeing the new feed and accept it into its diet. Of course all pellets must be fresh. Manufactured pellets always have a freshness date stamped on their packaging.

Some professionals still feel that pellets are not adequate for a chinchilla's full daily nutritional requirements and they mix their own feeds adding specifically measured quantities of such things as wheat, bran, barley, millet, linseed, dietary calcium, feed salt, skimmed milk powder, and herbs such as hip, peppermint, sage, mallow, etc. Up in the Andes, chinchillas ate varieties of grasses and seeds. Their artificial diets are the results of years of study and experimentation by experts. Unless you have consulted an expert in the field of raising chinchillas, you should avoid such experimentation and stay with the diet your pet store operator has established.

Since chinchillas are night creatures, a common practice is to feed them in the early evening, just prior to their most active periods. This feeding time may vary. Since chinchillas maintain habitual schedules, it is wise to learn exactly what feeding time they are used to and continue it. It has also been observed that some chinchillas will develop convulsions when fed a few hours past their normal feeding time. Also, if late feeding persists, some animals begin biting their own fur, which could lead to a whole series of other health difficulties. Naturally, the chinchilla's water supply should be made available at all times.

The chinchillas' diet of dry food increases their need for fresh water. Early chinchilla ranchers originally believed that the animals could go for long periods of time without any drinking water at all. Subsequent observations and study have shown this belief to be completely false. Chinchillas need water just as humans do. While fresh spring water is the best type for any animals, it is sometimes difficult to obtain. Many chinchilla breeders have expressed concerns regarding fertility problems from the chlorinated water from many metropolitan water supply systems. Since this is the water source that most pet owners have to rely upon, it is best to boil it prior to giving it to the chinchilla and add a pinch of sea salt.

Remember that it is very important that the water bottles be replenished daily. The chinchillas receive fresh water with their evening food. Unused water must be discarded at each feeding. Each filling of the water bottles must be preceded by a thorough rinsing, and twice a week the bottles should be thoroughly cleaned to remove any algal growth. The best way to

Pellets, hay (either loose or cubed), and water will fulfill the nutritional requirements of your chinchilla.

Dry uncooked breakfast oatmeal will be a special treat for a chinchilla. Reduce the amount of the regular ration to compensate for such treats.

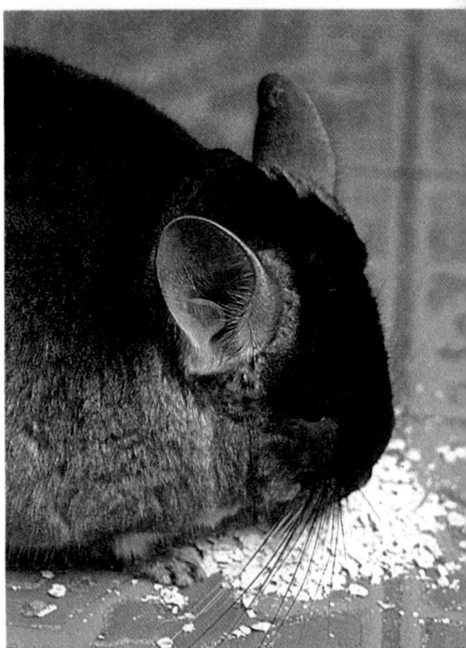

achieve proper cleaning is by using mild dish washing detergents followed by a thorough rinsing with clean water. Algal growth on the sides of the water bottle must be removed. The bottle stoppers must also be cleaned and chewed tubes replaced regularly.

It cannot be emphasized enough that cleanliness is of paramount importance. Any carelessness while cleaning the drinking bottles can easily lead to diseases and mortalities. Suggestions to use open drinking containers such as bowls, dishes and cups must be categorically rejected. Animals, like humans, like to drink clean, fresh water from clean containers.

With experience you will learn to distinguish good hay by touch, sight, and smell.

Again, if you need to change their feeding time for any reason, do so gradually. If they have to be left unattended for a few days, this can be done as long as an adequate supply of food and water is easily accessible. They will not overeat and will enjoy their meals at the same time each day on their own. Avoid making this a regular practice, however. While the feed will not go bad over a short period of days, having the feed dishes constantly full gives you no barometer as to the regular eating habits of your pet. Observing these habits gives a good indication of oncoming health problems since a chinchilla will change these habits at the onset of any illness. Adhere to the regular feeding schedule as often as possible.

A healthy adult chinchilla should be fed one or two heaping tablespoons of solid pellets per day. Since chewing on hard surfaces aids the chinchilla's tooth development, it is not a good idea to crush the pellets before feeding them to your pet. Being able to chew and break their food apart on their own helps prevent many possible dental problems in the future. This is true even in younger chinchillas. Their teeth are always growing and they need that dental exercise.

Many chinchilla owners feed their pets a helping of hay twice a day, morning and evening. If this is not done in excess, it appears to be a healthy practice. If there is too much hay provided, the active chinchillas will tend to pull out more than they can eat, compacting the uneaten portions on the floor of their cage. If this hay lays there for a time, it could become soiled by the pets or moldy. While it is rare that they will eat this compacted material on their floor, it is a possibility and a danger since moldy or soiled hay could develop fungus.

Loose hay and pellets utilized on a chinchilla ranch. Chinchilla ranchers are very particular about nutrition. One can not expect quality furs from undernourished chinchillas.

While the manufactured pellets available today are the main course for the chinchilla, hay was the previously recognized main staple for chinchillas. Hay provides roughage, which is defined as any coarse or tough food material containing a high percentage of indigestible elements. This material helps to break down other food and aids in the digestive process. There are also other foods which help to provide a healthy, balanced diet, but hay is still an important ingredient. Unlike the ease of supplying your chinchilla with pellets, the proper hay is often difficult to obtain. The hay cannot be from chemically-sprayed fields. Freshly harvested hay is not good for chinchillas since the fermentation process has not had time to be completed. The hay must be dried and cured to prevent mold development. Chinchillas cannot tolerate mold and cannot regurgitate contaminated food. If such moldy hay gets into their systems, it could cause major health problems.

The standards for safe and healthy hay for chinchillas are very specific. Many breeders and ranchers harvest their own or buy it directly from farmers. They must know these standards and be careful to grow and select only the proper types of hay for their animals. While pet owners should be aware of the dangers the wrong varieties of hay might present, they should rely on the knowledge and expertise of their local pet shop owners since this is where they will, most likely, obtain their pellet and hay supply.

One of the concerns chinchilla breeders mention is that of using hay which has not just been dried on the ground, but dried on outside stacks for a week. This hay has been dried by both the sun and by internal ventilation, inhibiting the growth of fungus, which can cause quite a number of health problems, especially in younger chinchillas.

Timothy hay, a coarse feed with long, cylindrical spikes, and oats harvested and dried shortly after they flower are often used by some chinchilla breeders, but these types of hay and straw are rarely dried under the exacting conditions needed. If you are not certain of the process used to prepare these types, you may be using food which may possibly present the danger of fungus development. If harvested hay *is* obtained directly from a farmer by the pet owner, similar caution should be taken to make certain any hay is from the first cut of the season and grown in a lean type of soil. You should also be certain that the hay was harvested when it did not rain.

Any hay fed to your chinchilla must always be dry and brittle enough to be easily crushed in your hand. If you have a supply of hay to store, it must be kept dry. In periods of high humidity hay absorbs the moisture, becomes tough, and loses most of its crispness. If a chinchilla feeds on inferior quality hay, diarrhea often occurs. In fact, if diarrhea does occur in your chinchilla, making certain its hay supply is dry should be the first step in altering the condition rather than immediately medicating the animal's problem with any kind of constipating agent. We note this problem here since it is a common error among novice chinchilla owners.

Hay can be dried for a couple of days in a cardboard box near a radiator or suspended over the top of a stove (where neither basket nor hay will catch on fire), or outside spread out where it may be redried by the rays of the sun. If the outside method is used, make sure other animals do not have access to the area since hay contaminated with urine or feces may be dangerous or fatal to your pet.

If the proper type of loose hay is not available or too difficult to find, alternatives can be found in your local pet store. Dried and pressed cubes of hay, often called mini-bales, are one to two inches long, an inch wide, and are made from alfalfa. They are pesticide-free, grown in areas with low humidity, and are carefully dried and cured. Some breeders have expressed a concern over using any form of alfalfa hay since it is considered a high-energy food. Chinchillas in the wild have adapted to a low-energy diet. These breeders prefer good quality meadow hay or highland or alpine pine hay. Again, this is mainly a breeding concern and the hay cubes should be adequate and safe for a pet chinchilla. However, to be sure, consult your own local pet store owner.

Since hay cubes have been pressed and shaped into hard blocks, they also provide still another chewing surface for your pets. Fifty-pound bags of hay cubes are available, but unlike the pellets, they retain their nutritional value for a greater period of time. They must be stored in a dry place where mold is not allowed to develop. They should not be stored directly on a concrete floor, where any dampness could cause mold. Smaller bags are available at pet stores and may be more practical for a pet owner.

The bales can be broken into several parts and fed over a period of days. The chinchilla will only eat what it wants of the hay and use the remainder of the bale as a plaything. If this happens, be certain to clean up the remains of the bale as soon as possible. Once broken apart, the hay in the cubes is susceptible to mold or contamination caused by the animal's waste.

If your chinchilla has been enjoying loose hay and you want to switch it to mini-bales (or vice versa), there is no problem such as there might be with different chinchilla pellets.

A chinchilla getting salt from a salt spool. The need for salt will depend on the nature of the regular food taken, according to whether sufficient salt is present or not.

Chinchillas love hay and will eat it in both forms with equal relish.

There are substitutes such as hay replacer. There are a few reasons such a substance may be used, one of which is a pet owner's possible allergy to hay. Hay replacers contain the roughage needed as well as vitamins, protein and various minerals. It is available in large bags and, similar to the mini-bales, it will last for a considerable period of time before losing any of its basic food value. Hay replacer should not be mixed with pellets since the chinchilla will pick out one and eat the other.

While we've stressed the importance of feeding your chinchilla at regular times during the day, one aspect of owning any sort of pet is the fun of feeding it special treats. There are certain treats which are not only fun to feed your pet, but they can do it a world of good as well. Remember that feeding your chinchilla is a great responsibility since your pet depends on you for all of its nourishment. While supplementary treats are fun to give, they are subject to similar exacting specifications as the animal's regular feed.

Pellets will normally provide the

chinchilla with everything it needs to maintain a healthy diet along with its normal hay and water consumption. With a healthy pet, you should not have to feed it extra vitamins or salt. In the past, owners often provided a salt spool for the animals. Now, since the newer pellets contain the minimum sodium and vitamin requirements, such dietary additions are not needed unless your pet is ill and extra supplements are recommended by a veterinarian.

Extra nutrition in the form of treats may be "necessary" if your pet is recovering from an illness, experiencing a rapid growth spurt or is pregnant. Even if such supplements are not expressly *needed* both the chinchillas and their owners enjoy "treat time." Just as meals are scheduled regularly, treats should be at a scheduled part of the day as well. Choose only one treat at a time. Don't mix them together and don't mix them with other feed. A chinchilla will separate its food, picking one to eat and the other variety to throw around.

There are a number of specific chinchilla treats and supplements which are available at your local pet shop. Treats for other small animals might be suitable as long as they contain only seeds or pellets for herbivorous animals such as those prepared for gerbils.

There are some existing recipes for homemade treats, but you should consult your local pet store owner or

Vitamins in liquid form can be given directly through the mouth or incorporated in the daily ration of pellets.

Sunflower seeds are relished by chinchillas, but they are a rich food and should be given sparingly.

an experienced chinchilla breeder before concocting such mixtures.

To avoid making your pet overweight and lethargic, you should not serve it more than a tablespoon of any treat or supplement per day. If overfed on treats, the animal might have a tendency to ignore or eat less of its needed diet of pellets, hay and water. This basic diet is essential to its continued good health and life span. If you notice any such tendencies, you should discontinue any treats for awhile. Again, this should be done slowly, lessening the amount of treat per day until you've stopped altogether.

The time for treats should occur a good twelve hours after the regular feeding time. The supplement should have its own dish or cup apart from the regular feed dishes.

Sunflower seeds are popular among many chinchilla owners since not only do the animals like them, but they aid in giving the animals a shiny coat of fur.

The bark of apple trees is a popular treat, as long as you're certain they come from trees which have *not* been sprayed with any insecticides. Large apple tree branches are cut into smaller sections so that when the bark is eaten, the wood can be chewed to help the chinchilla's teeth. Along with apple bark, small pieces of the apple fruit itself are also often given as treats. Fruit tree bark is good as long as it is a seed-producing fruit. Fruits such as cherries or plums, which

If you feed your chinchilla any kind of green food, examine the droppings for any adverse effects. Some greens are laxative in character.

A double treat for your pet chinchilla will be time out from its cage and a handful of its favorite cereal food.

have a stone rather than seeds, should be avoided. Certain varieties of these might be poisonous to the chinchillas.

Probably listed on top of the list of favorite treats is raisins. Not only do chinchillas love raisins, they also aid in preventing constipation. The animals enjoy them so much that they are also good to use if you find the need to medicate your pet. A drop of liquid medication on a raisin or a pill stuffed inside will be consumed immediately by the eager little animal. One drawback might be in the fact that too many raisins can be fattening. Once or twice a week should probably be a safe limit for raisins.

Some owners like to leave sprigs of the greenery from acceptable fruit trees on the branches they give their pets to gnaw on. Celery is also given on occasion, but there is a controversary regarding green food fed to chinchillas. Some experts are strongly against using any variety of green food except for treating "fur biting." Some breeders who have fed green food to their herds report discovering loose feces and diarrhea which suggest certain kinds of digestive disturbances. Other chinchilla breeders are strongly in favor of a green food diet and report no problems. However, since there have been some questions raised, it might be wise for a beginner to stay away from these specific treats until they talk to an expert.

Chinchillas will often eat their treats slowly, sometimes taking a full day to gnaw away an apple wedge or a larger piece of fruit bark. If it isn't finished by the end of the day or by the next regular feeding time, the remainder of the treat should be removed from the cage so that mold or other contamination will not have the chance to set in.

The basic rule to remember when feeding your chinchilla is that it needs a diet of pellets, hay and water, that it should be fed this at a regular time every day and that if you make any changes, they must be gradual. All of the rules of feeding should be adaptable to your individual pet based on the recommendations of the original pet shop owner or chinchilla rancher.

Facing page: *Caged chinchillas on a chinchilla farm, especially future breeders, are given supplements to improve not only their health but also their disposition. Hand-feeding reduces their aggressive tendencies.*

Keeping Your Chinchilla Healthy

Chinchillas are tough little animals. Perhaps originally coming from the Andes has made them highly resistant to disease and other physical problems. If they have a clean environment and a steady, proper diet, they will remain healthy and playful for many happy years. There are, however, certain health problems which do occur on occasion. A conscientious pet owner should be both aware and prepared for such problems.

Chinchilla breeders are constantly concerned for their herd and are always on the lookout for infectious bacterial diseases. Epidemics among a breeder's herd could wipe out his entire chinchilla population. An overall vaccine has been available through veterinarians for quite some time. It can be administered to your pet at any age and will protect them from the more dangerous diseases that might attack. The vaccine is given in a series of two shots, a week apart, with an annual booster shot.

Since pet chinchillas usually enjoy such a closed and protected

Given the opportunity, healthy chinchillas will not hesitate leaving the cage. They are quick on their feet and catching them can be difficult.

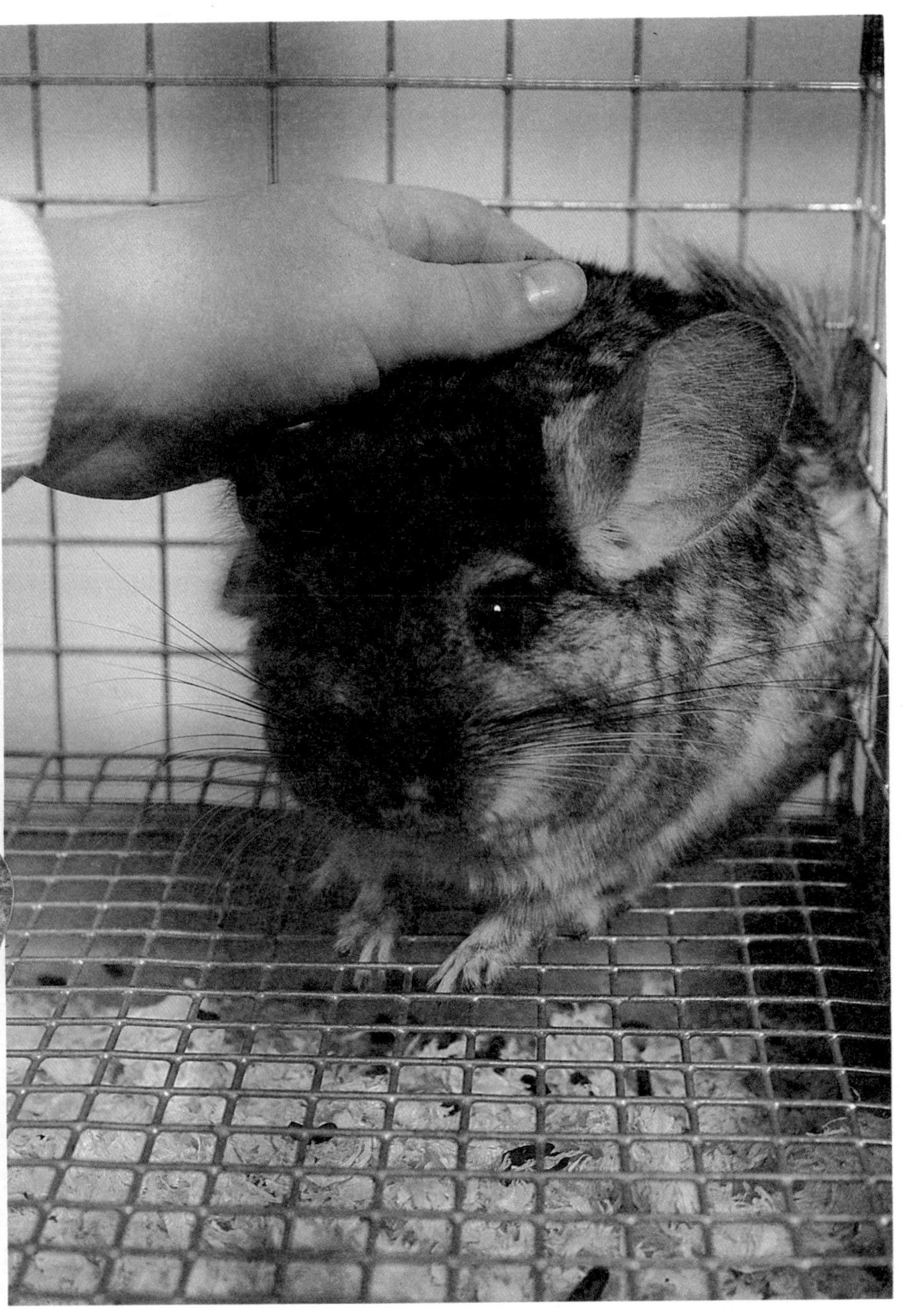

Chinchillas love to be petted on the head. Scratching the ear can calm a nervous chinchilla.

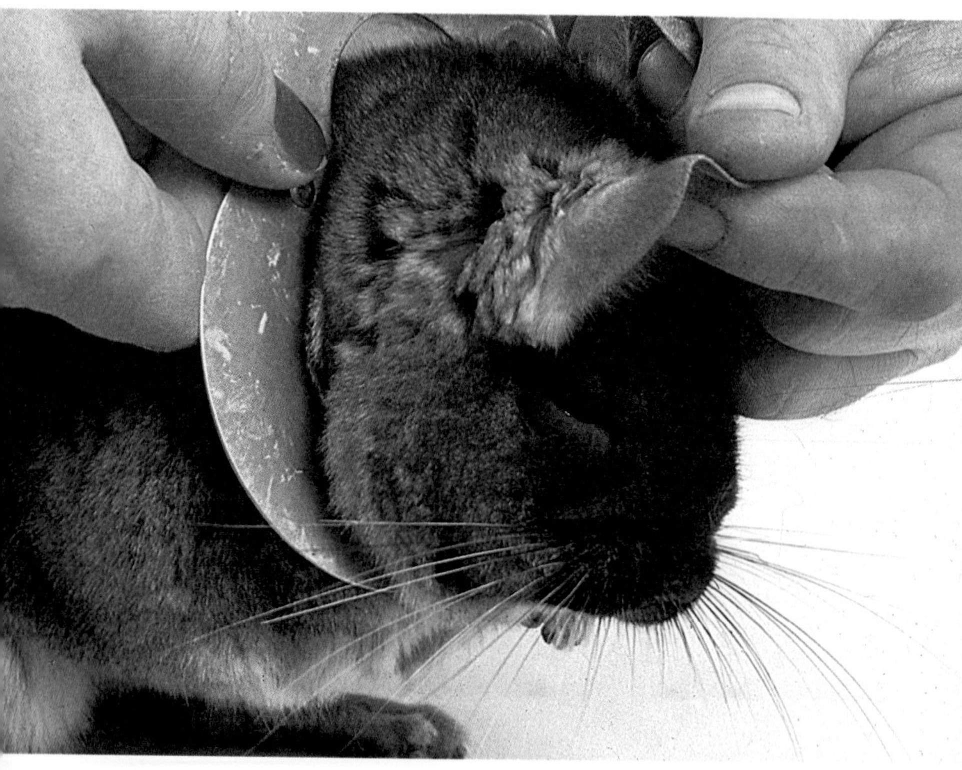

Ears that appear flushed and feel warmer than usual could indicate your chinchilla is feverish. Overactivity can raise a chinchilla's temperature but only for a short time.

environment, the majority of pet owners don't put their animals through any vaccination processes. Exposure to the causes of most diseases is nonexistent or extremely limited and they do not feel such precautions are necessary. Breeders and ranchers who are constantly introducing new stock, moving the animals or shipping them to different shows have more concern for exposure and often vaccinate their whole stock. Since such vaccination does protect against a great many diseases in chinchillas, pet owners might consider such an action a good idea. Any such vaccination program should be thoroughly discussed and administered by your veterinarian after a careful examination of your pet. The best insurance of your pet's continued health is to be totally aware of the common diseases that may show up and the actions you should take.

By carefully examining your pet on a daily basis and knowing what to look for, you'll have a better chance of noticing the onset of any disease very early. The earlier any ailment or disease is noticed and identified, the less difficulty you'll have in administering the proper treatment. If you have a specific worry, you should take your animal to the vet immediately. However, a simple external examination can be done every day. Your chinchilla will quickly become used to you and your handling of it. If a stranger tries to pick up your animal and finds it easy, and if the animal then sits listlessly in the newcomer's arms, it might be a sign of oncoming or existing sickness.

You should check all openings of the animal's body: its sex opening, its nose, its anus, its ears, its mouth and the areas around its eyes. When you look at its face be sure its eyes are bright and shiny.

A wire floor reduces the chance of your chinchilla's getting a fungal infection from damp bedding. A piece of board can be included to serve as a resting platform, too.

The eyes are a very important health barometer. Watery, teary eyes which appear dull are a definite warning sign. An infected eye will also have eyelids which are swollen and red with white matter collected around them. Sometimes, if such a condition is only discovered after it has reached an advanced stage, you might feel that it is beyond hope. However, even such advanced problems often are quickly cleared up by modern veterinary medicine.

Eye infections can be caused by a number of things, but the most common are brought about by dust or litter caught in the eye. Infectious bacteria may be the culprit if the animal's resistance is down after another illness or an unbalanced or improper feed combination. A

A heated nest box can be utilized for keeping sick chinchillas warm. The heat source is a light bulb of low wattage that can also be controlled by a thermostat.

petroleum based ophthalmic medicated jelly is the most common prescription for such conditions. This should be acquired from and initially applied by your local vet. If the condition is of the more advanced state, the veterinarian might recommend antibiotics as well.

Since it will probably take three or four days for any such medicated eye infection to begin to clear, you will probably have to continue application of the ointment at home. If this is the case, you should be certain to thoroughly clean and disinfect your pet's cage prior to returning the pet. Also, since eye ointments are sticky, you should remove the normal litter in the cage's bottom. The chinchillas will try to remove the ointment by rolling and tossing around. Particles could adhere to the ointment and cause more irritation or damage. A towel, cloth or newspapers are a better bottom covering during any healing process which requires ointment.

If there is no infection accompanying runny eyes, check the animal's temperature. An elevated temperature along with the eye condition might indicate pneumonia. There are special thermometers designed specifically for small animals, but you will probably want to get your vet's expert advice regarding the exact temperature. Nevertheless, there are a few ways to determine whether or not your chinchilla *is* running a fever. Just as a human, a chinchilla's normal temperature is 98.6 degrees. Without any special thermometer, you can see if the animal has a fever by touching and examining its ears. If they are pink or red in color and feel abnormally warm to the touch, then there is a high probability of a fever. Prior to this method of determining temperature, observe the position in which your pet has been sleeping. Sometimes, if the ears are tucked under the sleeping animal, the ears, warmed by body heat, may produce appearances similar to those described above. Wait a while after the animal has awakened before trying to determine an elevated temperature.

If you do suspect a fever, the animal will probably also appear listless. If this is the case, you should also listen carefully to its breathing. If it experiences difficulty breathing, makes a wheezing sound or shows a nasal discharge it might indicate a case of pneumonia or other respiratory illnesses. In a case of pneumonia, this causes unusual stress to the animal's circulatory system and heart. In fact, it is this kind of stress that is usually the direct cause of death in such instances. In most cases, you will require the services of a vet to treat pneumonia. Only a trained expert will know the exact type and needed dosage of antibiotics. If such *is* the case, you should also remember that you will most likely have to administer water to the stricken animal via a water dropper several times a day and make certain the animal is kept warm in a quiet place.

If the symptoms mentioned above occur minus any difficult breathing, your chinchilla might be suffering from the common cold. In such a case, all you need do is keep the animal warm and be certain it drinks plenty of water. Also, don't allow the animal to have a dust bath until the cold symptoms clear up. Continually examine the animal to make sure no pneumonia symptoms appear later on.

While pneumonia is not rare in chinchillas, it is more likely that watery eyes are a sign of a more common chinchilla difficulty such as dental problems. If you observe the animal pawing at its mouth or drooling when it eats, dental problems might be the cause. If such a condition has continued for a time, the animal might not have had the proper chewable foods and playthings to wear down its constantly growing teeth properly.

A mother chinchilla and her young. Healthy chinchillas have dry nostrils and breathe at an even rate. A yellow nasal discharge is certainly suspect.

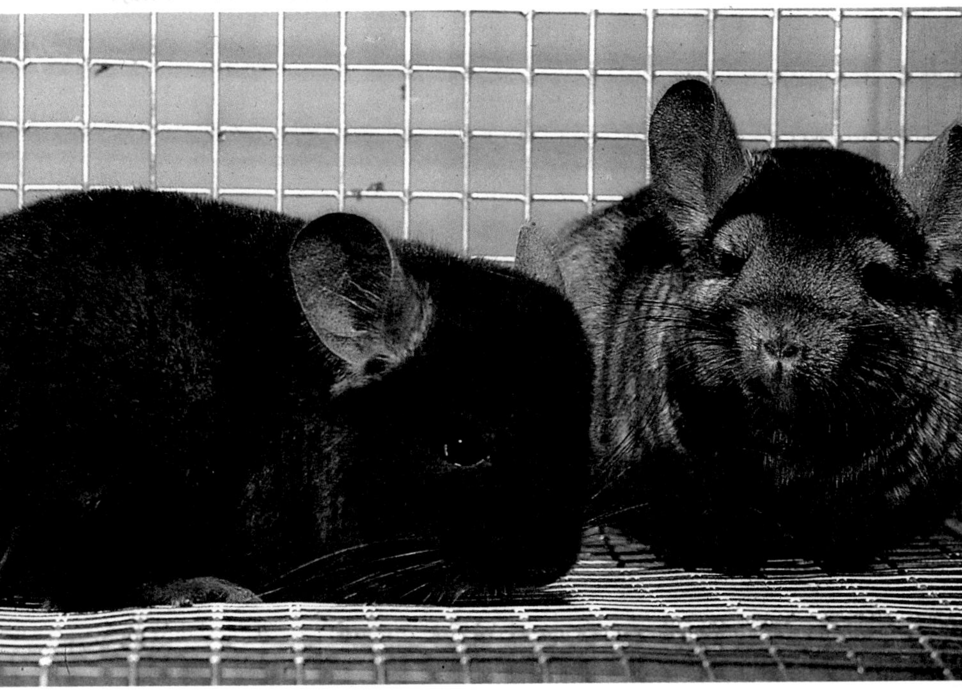

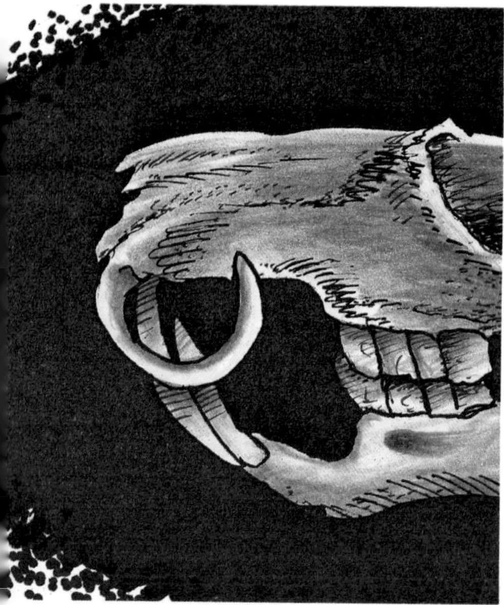

Illustration of a chinchilla skull showing incisors that have grown to extreme proportions.

Weight loss will also be a sign of improper eating habits due to dental problems. If the front teeth are clipped with a sharpened pair of nailclippers and watery eyes and chewing problems persist, the problem might be caused by spurs which have grown from the back teeth up into the eye sockets or down through the jaw. A veterinarian's x-ray can determine the exact difficulty. If these advanced problems occur (usually in older animals) and the pet can no longer eat properly, the humane action to take would be to put the animal to sleep to end its suffering. There is no permanent cure for many of these internal dental problems in chinchillas. Of course, most of the problems involving the front incisors can be prevented if the animal is always provided with something to chew.

Watery eyes may also be a sign of fungus. Fungus infections are most common during hot, humid and muggy seasons, but, depending on your pet's immediate environment, they could appear just about anytime. Sometimes fungus develops in damp hay or on an injured area of the animal's skin which has not healed properly. Some varieties of fungi make the chinchilla's fur fall out around its eyes and nose, exposing bright red or pink irritated skin beneath.

Fur breakage is a symptom of another fungus type, making the

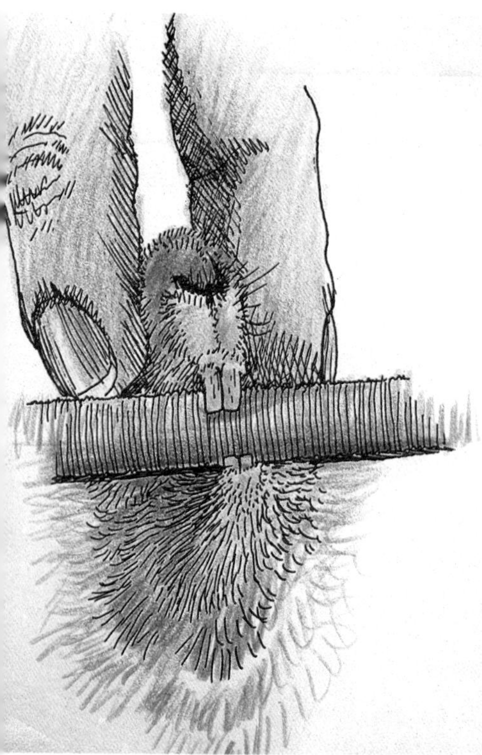

Jagged and uneven edges of the incisors can be filed smooth using an ordinary three-sided file.

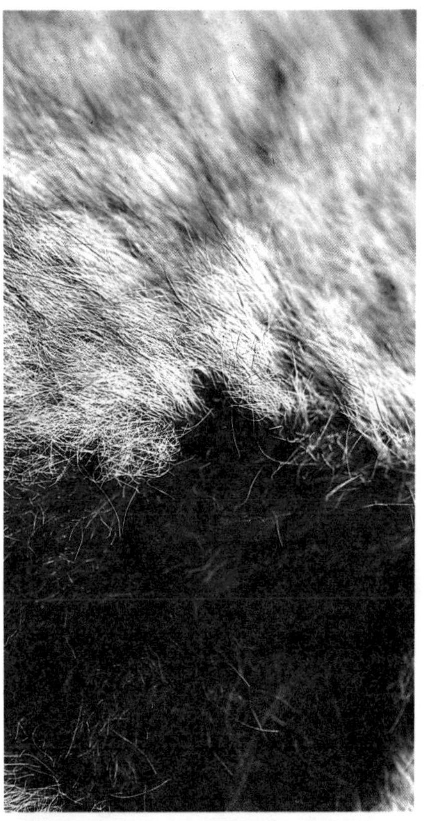

The exposure of the black-colored part of the hair shafts is an indication of fur biting. The light-colored tips have been bitten off.

animal's hair thin and shaggy-looking and causing its whisker ends to split and break at the ends on one or both sides of its snout.

The chinchilla will "help" you in curing these problems since a dust bath mixed with a tablespoon of a fungicide is the normally prescribed cure. While you should consult your veterinarian for specific fungicides, many owners have had their own successes against fungus by mixing in a heaping tablespoon of a foot powder for athlete's foot. Another remedy has been the use of one of the variety of powders used for fungus control in gardens. Cautions against using this latter variety have come up since some people have reported a high sensitivity to this powder.

If you have one or more chinchillas, you should treat them all for the symptoms even if it only appears on a single animal. This will halt the possible spread of the fungus. Many breeders mix the fungicide routinely into dust baths on a monthly basis as a preventative even if they have detected no signs of fungus infection. Fungus-related skin irritation should begin to clear up within a few days. New gray or white fur will return to the skin areas about a week after they have regained their healthy pink color. If the fur appeared broken and did not fall out, it will take longer to return to normal since it has to go through its normal growth cycle.

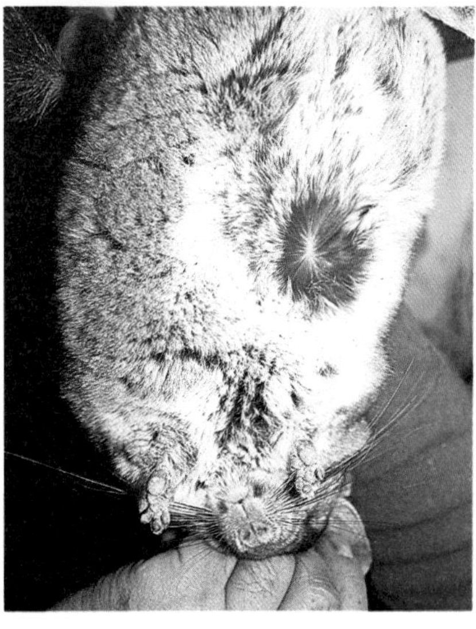

The quality of a chinchilla's fur is examined by parting the hair with a blast of air. There is no need to touch and handle the animal directly.

Some fur damage in chinchillas is not the result of fungus infection. Some chinchillas are fur biters, nipping their own hides. You can tell the difference by examining your pet's fur carefully. You should do this so that you're certain of the problem so you will not make the mistake of administering any medicine which is not necessary. Unnecessary medication could cause more damage and health danger.

If the area you are examining is matted, wet or looks as if it has been clipped short, then your pet has probably become a fur biter. No one has determined the exact reasons a chinchilla becomes a fur biter. Some chinchilla owners have stated their belief that the problem is inherited across a certain line of chinchilla. Some breeders believe damp, drafty or poorly ventilated conditions will cause the animal to become a fur biter. While the pet owner might not experience the problems, breeders have noticed an increase in the instances of fur biters in overcrowded conditions. Noise, irregular feedings, incorrect diets, all might have a correlation to the onset of fur biting. Fur biting is not considered a direct threat to the animal's health, but it is certainly

A chinchilla in the process of dusting its back—and visibly ecstatic about it.

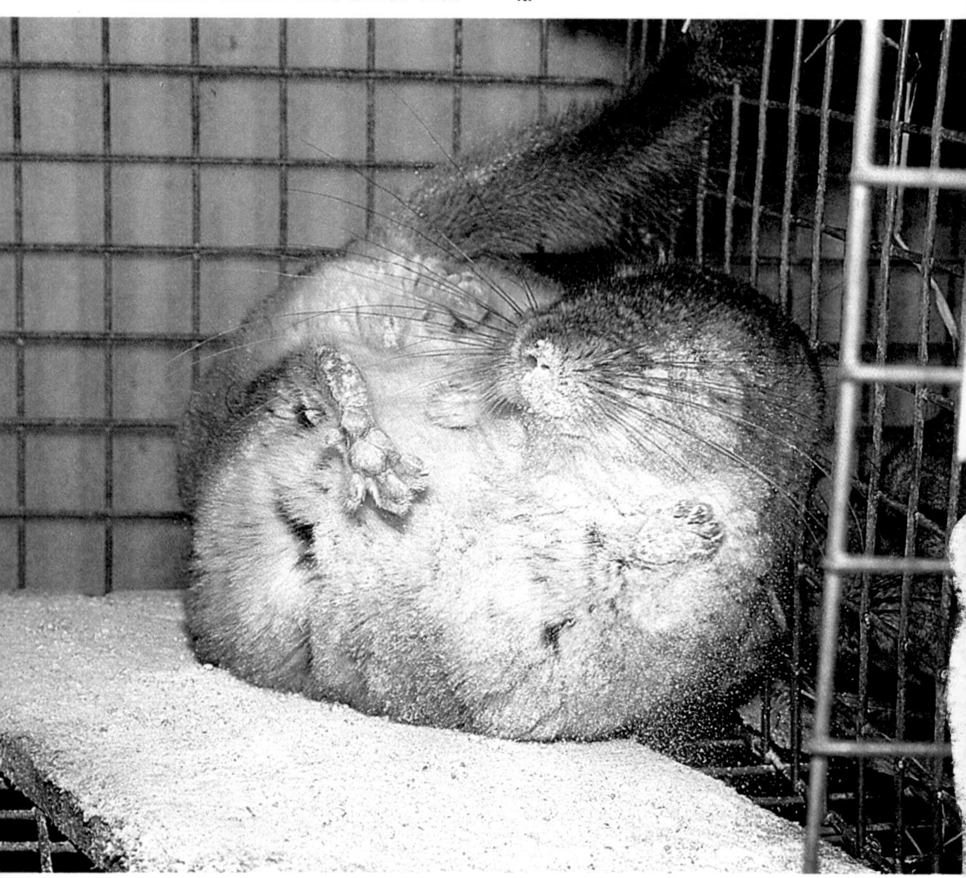

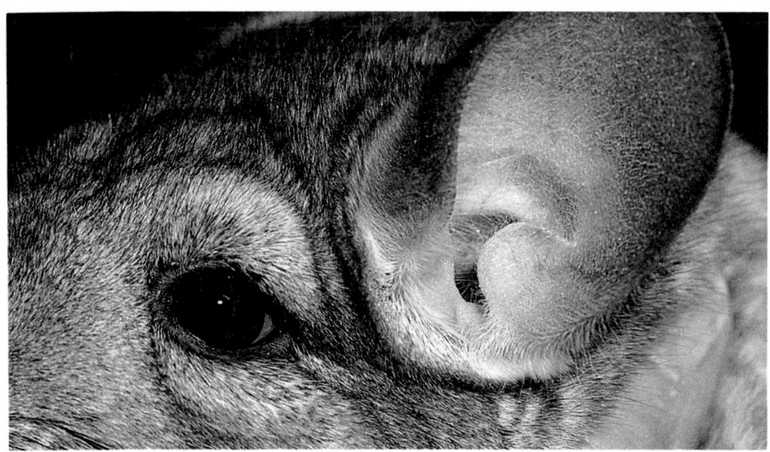

Any abnormality involving the ear of a chinchilla will be easy to spot. The ear is not heavily furred and the opening is quite wide.

damaging to the animal's appearance. Naturally, fur producers are always anxious to determine and eliminate any cause of fur chewing. Genetic causes aside, all of the above-mentioned problems lead to similar conclusions: Don't expose your chinchilla to any sort of prolonged stressful situations. They are sensitive animals and any kind of radical change in the routine will upset them greatly. They could very well express this stress by fur biting. If you can determine any stressful changes you may have brought upon your pet, change back to its regular routine, if possible, and the fur biting will probably stop. If any changes *must* be made, do so gradually, allowing the animal to accept the change slowly, preventing any build up of stress.

Examining the ears of your chinchilla should be a part of your daily examination of your pet. While ailments of the ears do not occur in the animals as often as, for example, eye ailments, any drainage from the animal's ear should be a cause for immediate concern. If you see your pet pawing at its ear or tipping its head to one side time and again, you should take it to the veterinarian as soon as possible. A chinchilla with an ear infection will also tend to walk in circles. The vet will probably clean the ear out and administer antibiotic drops. If you are required to continue the medication, you should take similar actions as you do with a medicated eye. You should thoroughly clean the cage, replacing litter with a towel, cloth or newspapers, and you should discontinue dust baths until the condition has cleared up completely.

While their closed environment usually protects them from minor cuts or scratches, you may find some while examining your pet. They need to be cleaned and treated with a simple antiseptic ointment which your veterinarian can recommend.

If you follow the prescribed diets for your pets, they should not experience any kind of seizures. Such fits, if they do occur, are usually the direct result of improper feeding. If you do find it happening, rush your pet to the veterinarian.

It will be best to refrain from spraying a chinchilla with insecticides; they may contain chemicals that it may be sensitive to. Always consult your veterinarian for the recommended medication for a particular parasitic infestation, if present.

Contrary to what you might believe to be normally brought on by a dietary cause, most constipation in chinchillas is due to such actions which might cause the animal to experience stress. Any kind of long travel or the changing of its location might bring on this condition as well. For this reason, constipation is a condition you should look for in any animal you've just acquired. Just bringing it home from the pet shop might produce enough stress to initiate constipation.

Dietary concerns are, of course, the other common cause, especially a sudden diet change. Many breeders and ranchers suspect a green food diet as being behind constipation problems as well. The most foolproof way to diagnose chinchilla constipation is by having its abdomen felt by the experienced and trained hand of a chinchilla expert or your veterinarian.

One highly recognized home preventive measure for constipation is to give your pet a small amount of Karlsbad salt mixed with its drinking water. The water bottle should be about half full and you should be certain that the chinchilla drinks it all. As with most cases of this sort, checking the animal's droppings the next day will aid you in determining if you need to give the animal a second dosage. This same solution is also very effective for a female chinchilla in a state of advanced pregnancy who suffers constipation just prior to giving, and following, birth. These chinchillas often tend to eat their afterbirth. This can cause some of the same digestive problems as mixed food in these animals. The Karlsbad salt solution also will aid in promoting the proper excretion for these animals as well. As you might expect, these measures are probably more of a concern to breeders and chinchilla ranchers, but, after checking with your own veterinarian, they will probably prove to be the safe and proper actions to take.

At times when you are trying to change a chinchilla's diet and have two types of pellets in its feed dish, constipation might be caused by the eating of this mixed diet. If you suspect that this is the case, the same remedy can be used, but with a slightly stronger mixture of the Karlsbad salt and drinking water. Also, in this instance you should feed the solution directly into the animal's mouth three times each day. Results should be evident in a day or two.

Although it has been used in the past (successfully in some cases), castor oil is not recommended for chinchillas suffering from constipation.

It is also important in the instance of chinchilla constipation that the chinchilla exercises. This can be

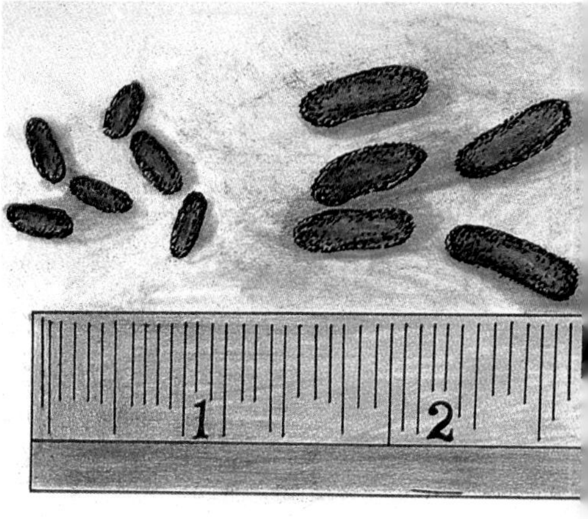

Be familiar with the appearance of normal droppings. They should be large, compact, and smooth.

An ordinary medicine dropper is very appropriate for administering small amounts of medication. There is less of a chance to spill the medicine.

Offering a slice of potato occasionally will be harmless. A whole one will possibly result in diarrhea.

done by letting it out of the confinement of its cage and allowing it the freedom to move around on the opened space of the floor. You can also increase the instances of dust baths and give the animal extra time for tossing and turning around in its dust.

Young chinchillas tend to eat too much. This will cause them to experience diarrhea. Terramycin powder can be added to the drinking water to correct this condition along with a normal feeding diet. Diarrhea experienced in older pets is usually the result of eating contaminated hay or food. If the direct cause can be discovered, it must be removed and terramycin should be added to the drinking water. Things should return to normal in a relatively short period of time. If not, consult your veterinarian.

If diarrhea or constipation conditions last over extended periods, the animal may be suffering from enteritis, an inflammation of the intestinal tract brought about by infection or irritating food. This may also be brought about if your pet has been on antibiotics for long periods of time. If this is the case, the animal will probably begin to refuse food and treats. It will also, most likely,

Allowing a chinchilla to roam in a room is beneficial. However, be sure that all the windows and doors are shut and the room free of hiding places.

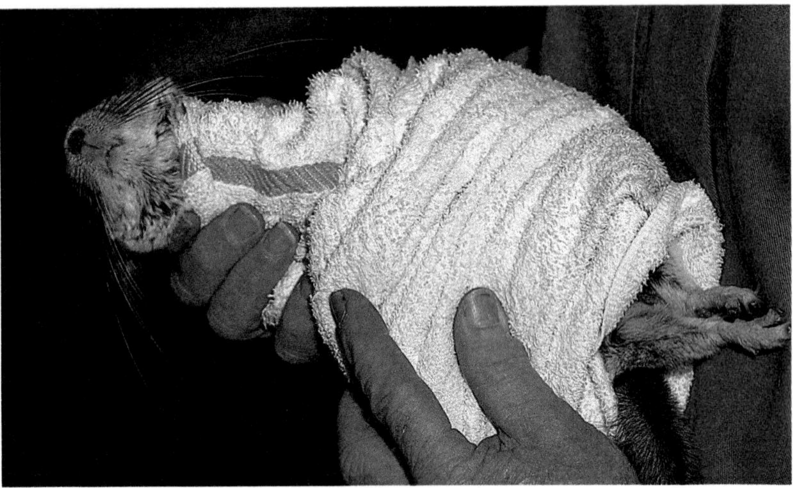

To restrain a chinchilla for transport is made easy by wrapping it in a towel, not too tightly but just enough to prevent escape.

have trouble walking and will tighten itself into a ball and just sit. If you observe this kind of unusual behavior, you should immediately take your pet to the veterinarian. The causes of enteritis come from different kinds of bacteria and tests will probably have to be made to determine the exact antibiotic needed to combat the condition. If possible, take some of the infected animal's droppings with you to the vet for the doctor to examine and for analysis.

Heat prostration might become a problem if your chinchilla's cage is not in a proper location and a heat wave occurs. If you find your pet gasping for air or lying on its side, then this is probably what has happened. In this case, move the animal to a cool room and give it plenty of cool water to drink. It might also be necessary to immerse the animal up to its neck in cool water until its temperature comes back down to normal.

If you do find it necessary to take your pet to the veterinarian, do your best to reduce what may be a stressful journey. Wrap your pet in a small bath towel. This will keep it warm, calm and restrained. This is a good practice when doing your normal daily examination of your pet as well.

There are many proper ways to medicate your chinchilla. Pills can be hidden in raisins or other treats while liquid medicines can be fed directly through an eyedropper. Your veterinarian and you will have to decide the best method for medicating an individual pet. It is best not to rely on medication that has to be sprinkled on feed or mixed with water. It is difficult to monitor the dosage that the chinchilla will actually take in these cases.

A clean, stress-free environment, balanced proper diet and continual observations are the watchwords for caring for your pet so it can enjoy a happy, healthy and lengthy life.

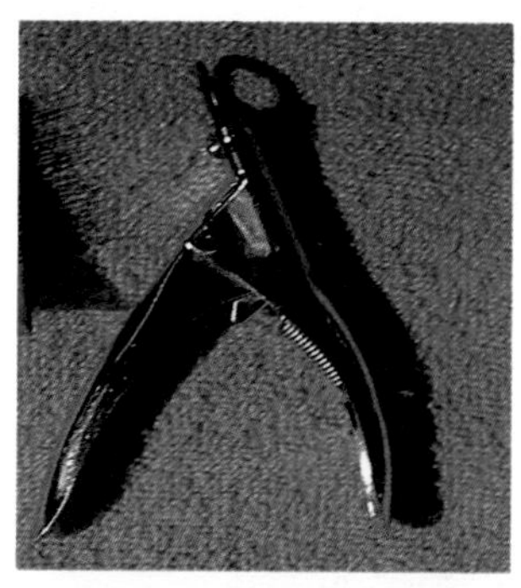

Toenail clippers are available at reasonable cost in most pet shops. Get the size appropriate for a small mammal.

Never trim the claws with an ordinary pair of scissors. There is a great chance of cutting the quick (supplied with blood capillaries), resulting in bleeding and an infected digit.

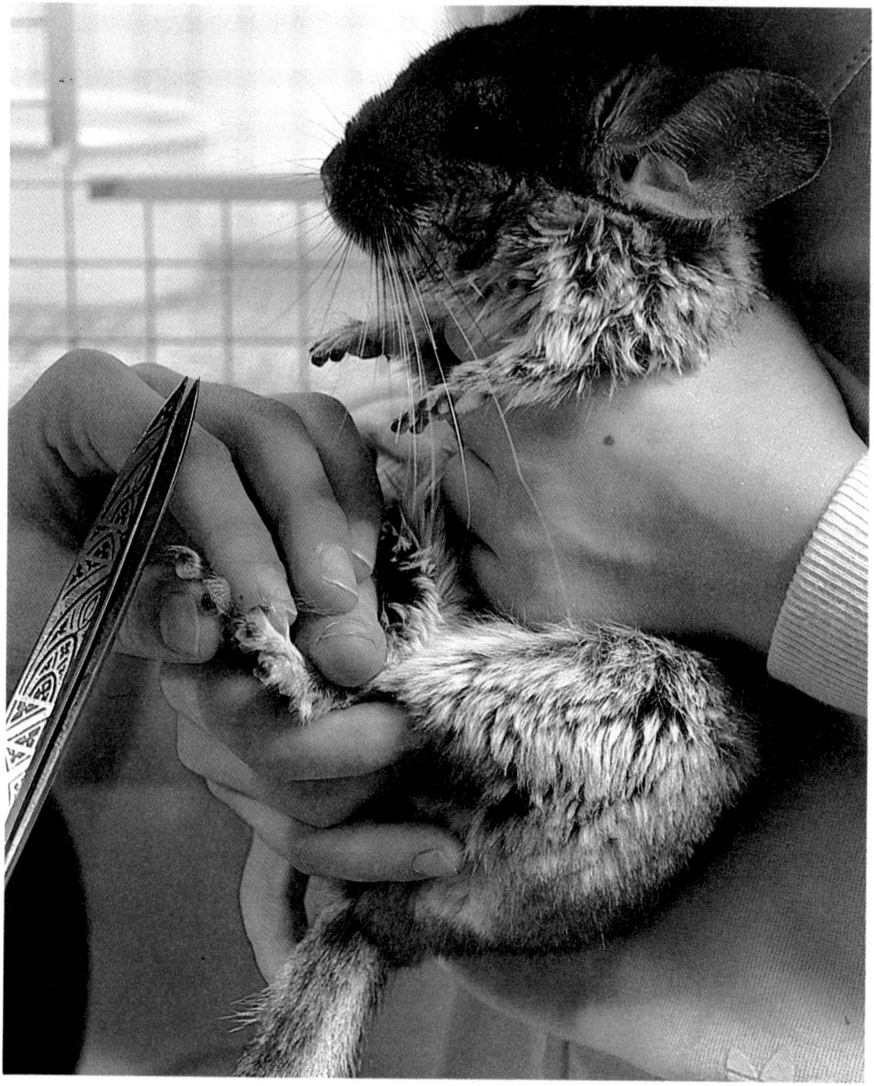

Breeding Pet Chinchillas

Breeding chinchillas for the fur trade is a big business. However, our subject is enjoying a chinchilla as a pet. For this reason, we don't intend to go into great detail on the breeding of chinchillas. The complex and exacting science of chinchilla breeding requires volumes of information concerning such things as selective breeding, mutations, linebreeding, etcetera.

A pet owner need not have such information at his or her fingertips. Such information is of value to a pet owner only as interesting background regarding a unique and beautiful pet.

On the other hand, there are a great many pet owners who would love the challenge of raising new pets. If this is your desire, then you need to learn some important basics regarding chinchilla mating, pregnancy, birth, infant care and weaning.

Unless you've initially bought a pair who have been previously caged together, the first thing you have to do with your single pet is to properly determine its sex . . . and then purchase the correct prospective mate. This may not be as easy as it sounds. The sex of newborn chinchillas is often difficult, especially for a layman, to determine. Even expert chinchilla ranchers have been known to make an error if they've made a quick notation at birth and have never gone back to double-check. Many experienced breeders have noted subtle external differences between buck and doe chinchillas so that they are able to determine which is which by a quick observation.

Normally, these experts point out, bucks have a smaller body shape than the does. The heads of the bucks are wider and bigger, but the bodies are smaller. The chinchilla female has two parallel rows of three nipples or teats on its abdomen, a total of six. The clitoris and the anus of the female are very close together and the horizontal vaginal opening is sometimes noticeable in between. Usually, however, this is very difficult to see. In contrast, there is a wide separation between the anus and penis of the male, normally 1 to 1.5 cm.

Chinchillas have no noticeable odor. We should, perhaps, amend that to say no noticeable odor to *humans*. Chinchillas can easily identify each other by individual odor. Before placing a male and female into a cage together as

View of the genital region of young chinchillas, a male on the left and a female on the right.

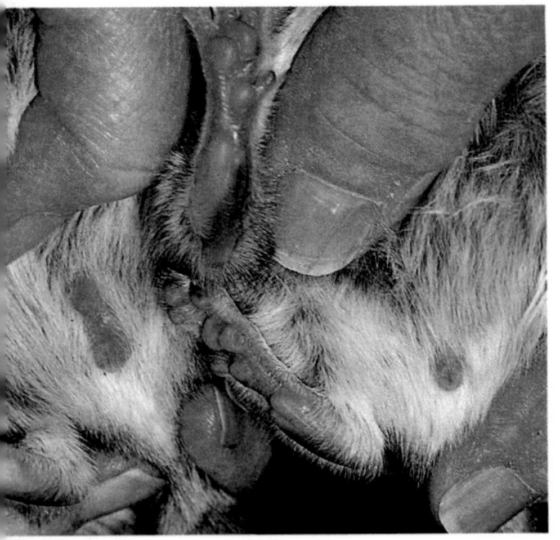

Facing page: *A female chinchilla and a male chinchilla (above) in one of the breeding cages of a chinchilla ranch. The male is free to move in a run with access to females caged in individual compartments.*

Closeup of the genital area of a female chinchilla. The transverse slit above the anus is the vaginal opening.

prospective mates, they should be given the opportunity to get used to and recognize each other's odors. This can be done by placing them in separate cages right next to each other. This should be done for at least a week before caging them together.

When you think they have become used to being near one another, place the buck into the doe's cage, being certain to be prepared to immediately observe their initial activities. This is extremely important since after the male has surveyed his new location, the two animals will probably engage in some playful tusseling. This normally takes the place of a friendly nibble around the face and ears. However, in some cases the two do not get along at first, and the playfulness can quickly turn into a biting fight. Aggressive females who reject the male will rear up and shoot urine at him. If any of these occurrences take place, separate the animals immediately.

The first thing that will normally take place when the male is first introduced into the female's cage will be for the buck to explore his new

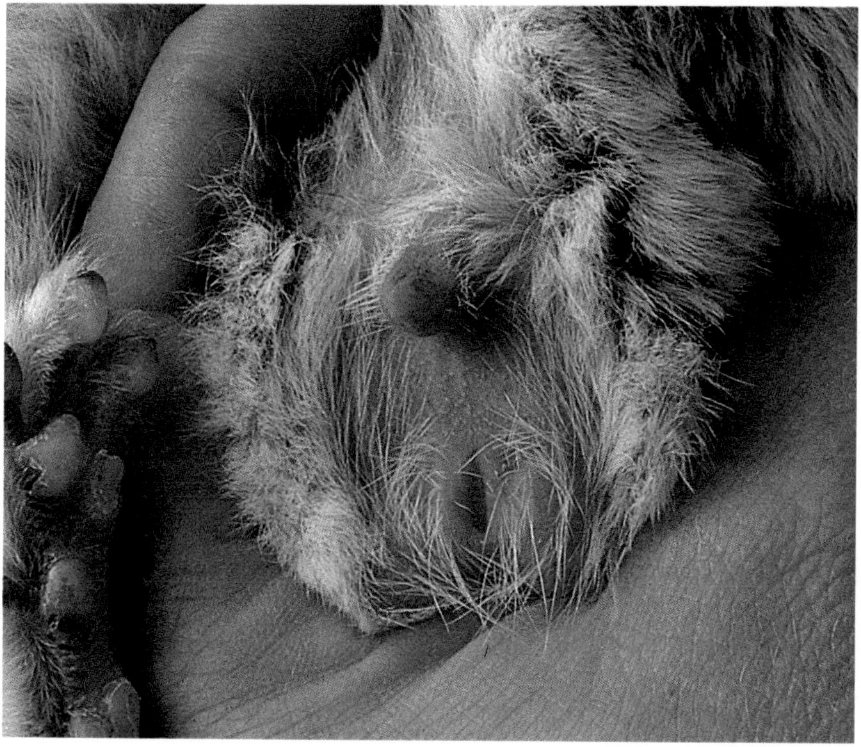

Closeup of the genital area of a male chinchilla. The protruding structure that is above the anus is the penis. It is separated by a good distance from the anus.

surroundings. He will usually be more interested in the four corners of the cage than in the female. He will chew on newly-found chew blocks and check out the feed and water before ever paying any attention to his prospective mate. On the other hand, the female will be curious about the newcomer in her cage and will follow the male around for a time.

If their initial meeting is unfavorable, try another week of side-by-side cages before placing them together again. They might have just needed additional time to get used to each other. If they continue to fight and bite when placed in the same cage, it will be necessary to replace one of them.

A male chinchilla mating with a young white female chinchilla. The male is generally separated after a successful mating.

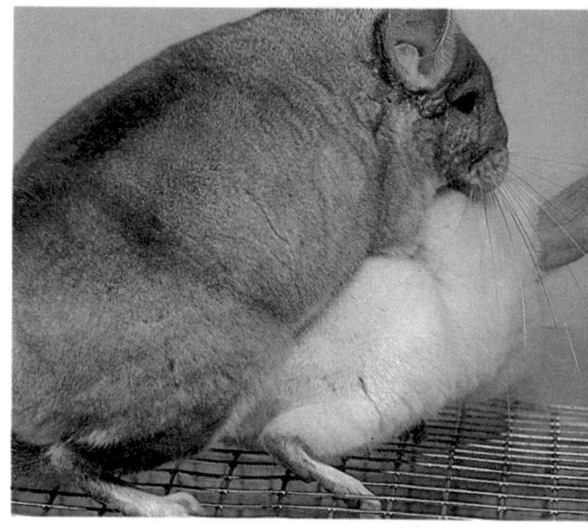

Usually, the more aggressive of the fighting pair is replaced for one who will be compatible. While incompatibility certainly happens between a pair of chinchilla, it is rare. Seldom do chinchillas completely reject a possible mate outright.

Chinchillas mate for life. Once they have decided to remain together, they seldom fight until the female comes into estrus. Even then, fighting sometimes never occurs.

If it is absolutely necessary to handle your pregnant chinchilla, be sure to support her rear end. Pregnant chinchillas grasped by the tail are known to abort spontaneously.

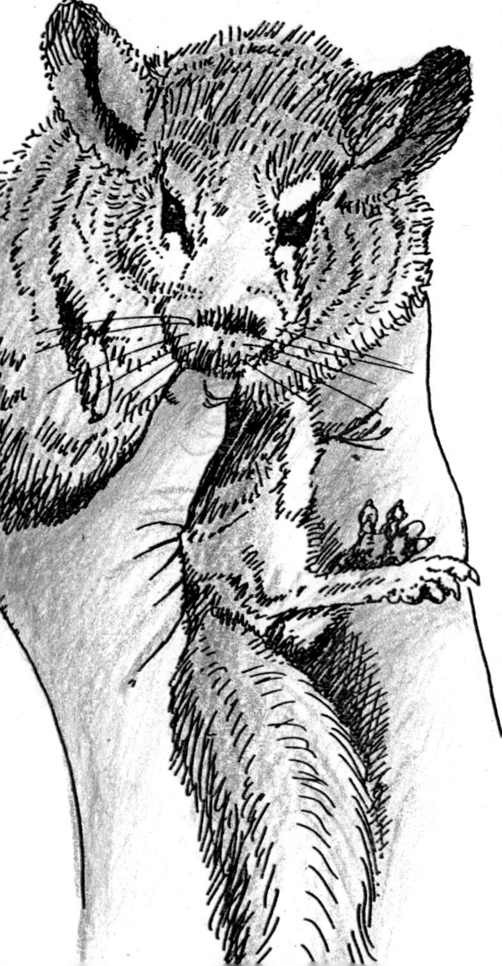

Chinchillas are very sensitive and are highly susceptible to stress. Since placing separate chinchillas together for the first time often initiates stressful situations, it may be awhile before mating attempts are made. For the male, it means becoming accustomed to a new home. For the female, it means sharing her space with a new creature. Both of these events could produce stress in your animals.

A female chinchilla becomes sexually mature at approximately seven to eight months old, with a 30 to 40 day cycle. She will not breed at all unless she feels secure with her surroundings. By carefully watching the male's increased interest in the female, you can usually tell when the doe is nearing the time when she is most receptive to the mating process. Nuzzling, attentiveness and sniffing by the male all increase, sometimes accompanied by tail wagging and sounds.

The female will eject a wax-like vaginal plug just before she is ready to breed and the male's more aggressive tendencies will increase because he is ready before the female.

If you want a breeding to take place, you should remove any potential hiding places from the cage. Often the female will hide from the male until her receptive period has completely passed.

Immediately after a breeding attempt has taken place, you will hear the male make a hiccupping cry. He will also eject a waxy substance into the female's vagina which will harden and temporarily hold his semen inside the female. At this time it is important to check the male to be certain he can withdraw his penis back into his protective foreskin. Occasionally, if the buck has had little or no experience, a hair ring will develop around the penis during copulation and he will not be able to

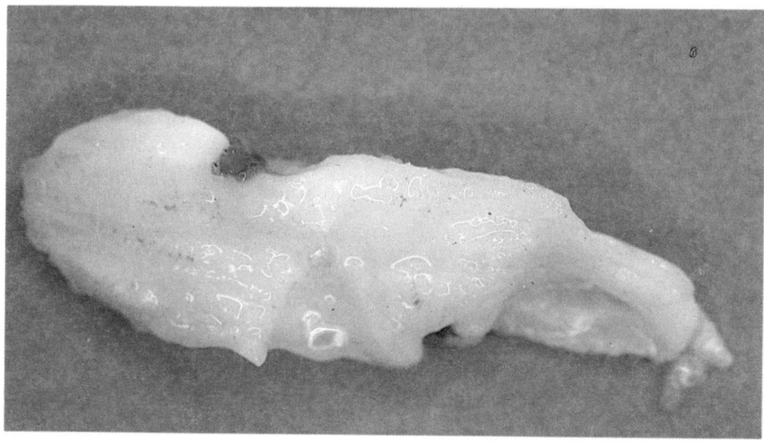

remove this himself. This will prevent the penis from withdrawing into the foreskin and it will cause the animal great pain and discomfort. If this is left unattended, the penis will become atrophied, causing agonizing death. If the buck appears lethargic and refuses to move or eat, it might be a sign of this problem. If you determine that this is the case, the hair ring must be dissolved in warm water and removed manually, using petroleum jelly as a lubricant if necessary. The organ is then very gently pushed into the foreskin once again. Close monitoring is needed aferwards to make certain the animal has regained full use. If swelling and redness appear, infection has set in and immediate attention and medication will be needed. Your veterinarian will be able to assist you here.

A freshly extruded vaginal plug. Once the plug has been extruded, the female can possibly mate again.

It is quite safe to leave the male and female together in their joint cage during the full 111-day term of the pregnancy. In fact, you should

An old vaginal plug is shrunken and dried out, but still recognizable and separable from the bedding material.

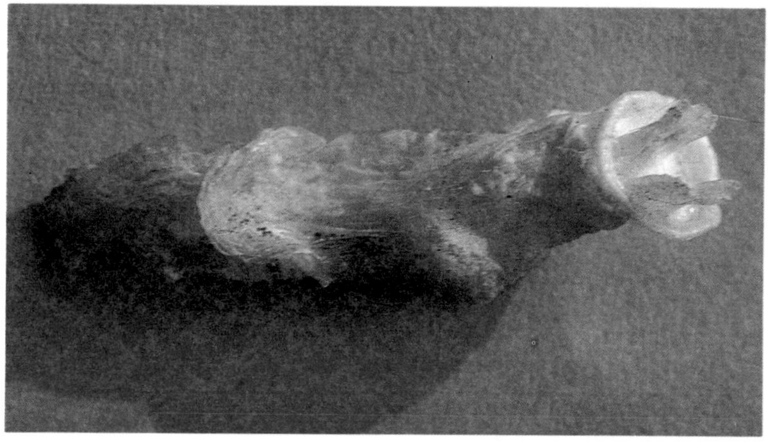

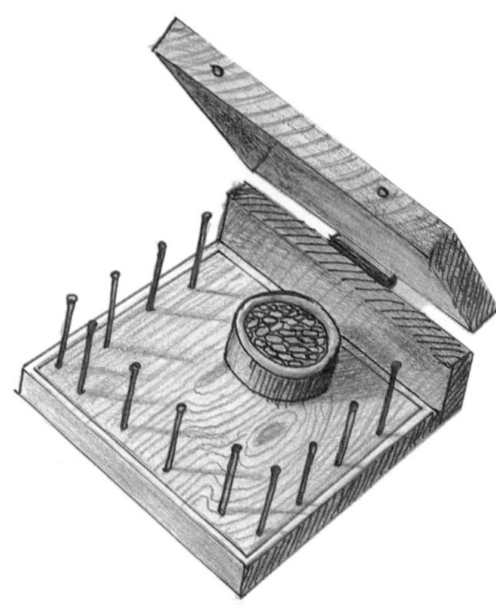

A baby creep is a device that keeps baby chinchillas apart from larger adults without having to move them into a separate cage.

not remove the female from her immediate and familiar surroundings. You should not handle the female during pregnancy even if you're tempted to weigh her or palpate her. You may increase her feed since she'll need a bit of extra nourishment, but do not be alarmed if she at times stops eating up to the point of losing weight. This is very normal for doe chinchillas.

The 111-day gestation period is very accurate give or take a day or two. If you plan ahead, you should know approximately which day the female will be giving birth. On that day, you must be certain not to allow the mother to take a dust bath. It is virtually impossible to assure a completely bacteria-free dust bath. Letting her take one would risk contracting womb or vaginal inflammations. Also, you might notice that on or immediately before this day, the female will begin taking in larger volumes of water and less food. Thus, the appearance of soft droppings, repeated stretching, and periods of time when the expectant mother just lies quietly are all signs of impending birth.

There is no need to aid female chinchillas during labor. Instincts take over completely. Birth usually takes place in the early hours of the morning. Initially, the female stretches and makes mournful laboring sounds. The fluid from the sac around the young will be discharged. The labor lasts only a short time and she will soon give birth. Most chinchilla births consist of twins, but triplets are not unusual. Multiple births actually take place over a period of hours.

The mother will gently birth the young with her teeth, cleaning and drying each baby with her own fur. It is highly unusual for a mother chinchilla to ignore any of its newborn. If this does happen, however, take the kit and immerse it in warm water up to its neck for a short time while massaging it gently. It should revive soon and you can wrap it in a warm towel or heating pad until it is ready to be returned to its mother.

The mother will deliver one placenta for each kit. It is normal for the female to eat the afterbirth, and when she does so, it is a sure sign that the birth has been completed. If you see blood on the mother's nose and on her forepaws, it is a clear indication that the afterbirth has been passed and eaten.

It is perfectly safe to keep both parents with the newborns, but the mother will most likely go into heat within the 24-hour period after giving birth. Since nursing one litter and carrying another simultaneously is very tiring for the female chinchilla, it is not a good idea to allow them to mate again right away. Remove the father, returning him after a few days.

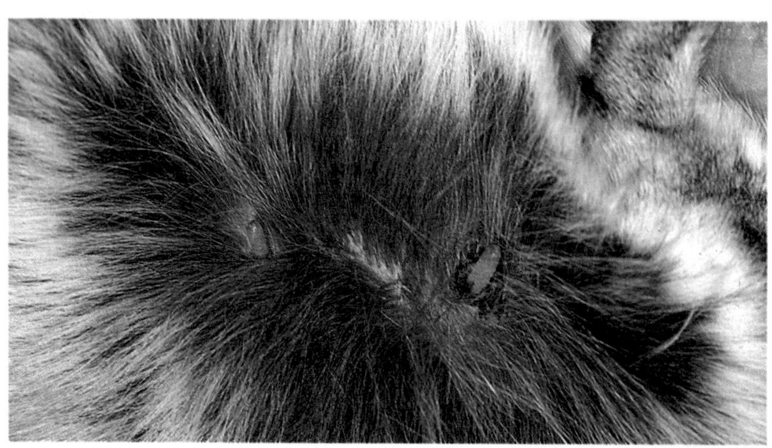

Unless the fur is parted, the nipples of a female chinchilla are not visible.

A beige female and a brown velvet male chinchilla. Being variable in color, mutations are graded according to the shade of color produced.

A chinchilla mother can adequately nurse a small litter.

Since chinchillas are born with a full set of teeth, it is usually necessary to clip or file them down before allowing them to begin nursing. The mother will not object if her babies are handled, so this should be easy to accomplish; of course no attempt should be made until you have received exact instructions from another chinchilla owner or your vet. This filing also prevents the very active young from harming each other since they sometime tend to scrap among themselves before choosing a nipple on which to nurse. Chinchilla mothers do not lie down to nurse like rabbits or cats. After a few hours, they raise up on their hindquarters and allow their young access to their teats. The young are born with about a 12-hour supply of nourishment, so they probably will not begin to nurse for about a half a day after they are born. If the litter is a large one, some breeders suggest letting the young nurse for only about two hours at a time for a week or so before allowing them to remain with the mother indefinitely.

After approximately six to eight weeks of nursing, the mother will initiate the weaning process. You will notice that by this time the young chinchillas will probably be drinking water at a normal rate. Once completely weaned, they must be carefully monitored to make sure they are not overeating. Overfeeding young chinchillas is one of the leading causes of mortality among these animals. They should, at this early age, be receiving only about half the amount of a normal adult chinchilla. Monitor them carefully, checking feces and other vital signs until they are fully grown at about five or six months. At this point, they can receive full rations.

Even though the young may seem completely weaned, it is a wise precaution to check the mother a few days later to see if she is still producing milk. If this is the case,

Grooming her young keeps a mother chinchilla busy. Be sure to provide the young chinchilla the opportunity to take a dust bath, or it may never learn to do so.

Newly born chinchilla, 2 minutes old, has eyes that are already opened.

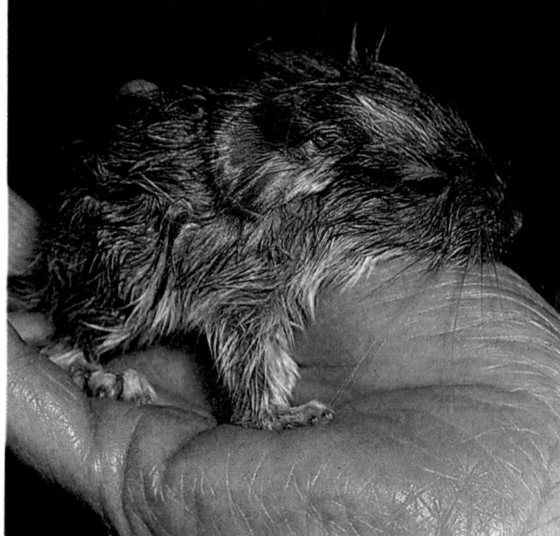

The same baby chinchilla an hour later.

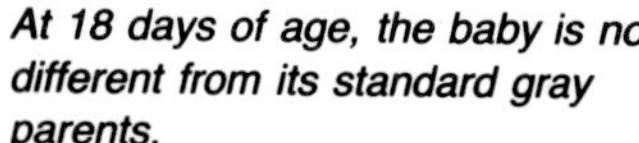

At 18 days of age, the baby is no different from its standard gray parents.

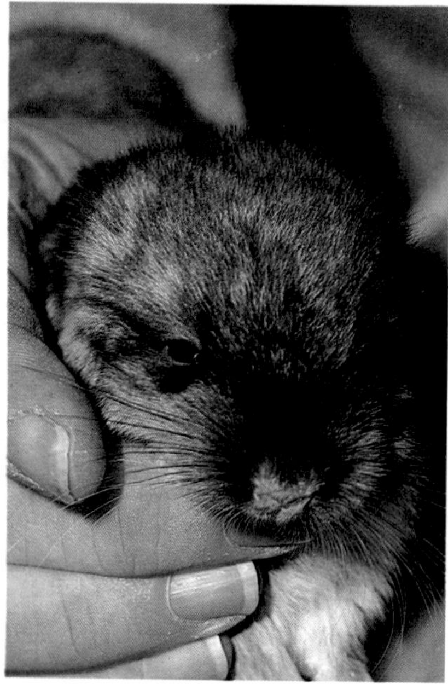

return the young to her for an additional nursing or two.

A mother chinchilla should be given at least a month before she breeds again. During this time the owner should check her habits carefully, making certain she returns to the routines of behavior and diet that she exhibited before becoming pregnant. Only after this time has passed and after you're certain she's healthy should you attempt to mate her again. Also remember that even if you want her to mate again, she may not agree. If she appears unwilling, just allow more recovery time.

If you're excited about raising chinchillas as pets, then this will prepare you for watching and aiding their further development as they become mature animals. As a pet owner, you've acquired your animals for companionship and for play. It's time to learn something about handling the chinchilla as a companion and a playmate.

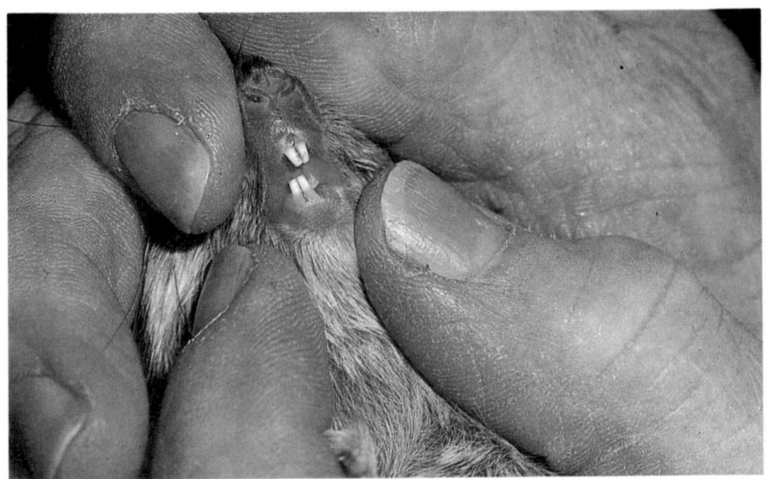

Born with full dentition, this hour-old chinchilla has well formed white teeth. The yellow normal color develops later.

If you intend to keep a chinchilla for a pet, handle it as early as possible and regularly. Remember that a frightened chinchilla sheds hair as a defense reaction.

Although nocturnal in habit, chinchillas (especially young ones) are active part of the day, feeding, chewing their toys, and playing with each other.

We assume that your desire to own a chinchilla for a pet is similar to the desires of traditional cat and dog owners: to have a companion you can play with for sheer enjoyment and fascination. Since chinchillas do not have the domesticated history of dogs and cats, their handling, while having similarities with traditional pets, takes some special considerations and cautions. If you keep these things in mind, then the enjoyment of owning a pet as unique and unusual as a chinchilla will be multiplied.

The playfulness you'll see in a young chinchilla remains with the animal throughout its life. Adults and kits alike enjoy exploring, nibbling, running and jumping. However, as each animal grows, the degree of this playfulness may change due to environment or health reasons. The first thing you should do, without regard to the chinchilla's age, is to get acquainted. If your pet is used to you and its immediate surroundings, it will soon have no fear about being petted, touched, lifted and held.

To allow your pet to get to know you, you have to let the animal utilize its senses. First among these is its sense of smell. You must extend your hand into the animal's cage and allow it to smell and sniff you. You should not make any sudden or quick movements and don't try to pet or catch the animal initially. Some animals won't mind being picked up right away, but you have to know their history before attempting this. If yours was in a pet shop for a time where the owner allowed previous prospective buyers to pet the animal, then it will probably take easily to you. If it is a young animal who has observed its mother being handled without harm, then it will probably do likewise. If your animal appears fearful at first, then the slow approach with the hand is the best method of introducing yourself to the animal.

Once your hand is in the cage the animal will examine this new intruder by sniffing. It might nibble a bit, so be ready for it and don't flinch. The sudden movement could easily terrify the animal. After the initial contact the animal will retreat to a corner of its cage to ponder over what it's just learned about you. In a few minutes it will return for a second look.

Eventually, it will consider your hands as part of its world and will actually sit down on them. Eventually, it will want to explore

Facing page: *A tame chinchilla senses by smell the person it trusts. Regular handling must be exercised to reinforce the taming process.*

Only someone experienced in handling chinchillas should try managing more than one animal at a time. Imagine having to chase chinchillas running in different directions!

further and start crawling up your arm. This, however, will probably not start to happen with animals not completely used to human handling. Animals who exhibit initial fear need to associate your hands with something positive. This is why it is a good idea to end the encounter by offering your pet a small treat. It's good to do this at the end of such encounters since doing so when you start out will cause the animal to spend all of its time with you searching for additional treats. Treat time and playtime should be separate events. If you do them on a regular schedule, the chinchilla will soon recognize and anticipate when you plan to do each one. They are, after all, creatures of habit.

When the animal is completely used to your hands, sitting on them and crawling up your arms, it should be prepared for you to catch it, hold it and remove it from the cage. Once removed, you'll note that it will probably be more interested in the new surroundings than in you or your hands. The animal has a strong curiosity, so this is quite natural. If you allow it to satisfy its curiosity (up to a point; don't allow it to endanger itself by unsupervised exploring), it will be willing to be lifted in your hands again, anticipating the scheduled treat. After a while, if you maintain this rigid schedule you might even find the animal waiting near its cage door for you to begin the playtime.

Chinchillas are quite intelligent. Their intelligence level has been compared to that of a squirrel. Anyone who has observed a squirrel will realize that the animals are very clever and can be trained to do tricks and follow scheduled behavior patterns. Chinchillas can sit up and beg, come when called, "speak," jump and do a variety of other tricks that delight both the owner and the animal. Training them can be easy by using the "reward method" as is common with cats and dogs. Treats for which the chinchillas have shown a preference can be used as the reward for performing a specific action.

Chinchilla breeders usually identify their female stock as soon as their sex is determined by placing on each a breeding collar as seen on this female beige chinchilla.

Similar to cats, chinchillas like to be scratched around the back of the ears and under their necks and chins. To a lesser degree, this action of nuzzling with the animal can be used as a "reward" for a "job well done " to aid in training. You shouldn't make playtime into a "training session," however. Constant demands on the animal might produce stress, which is a condition that should be avoided at all times. As we've noted before, many disease paths are opened if the animal experiences too much stress. If your pet starts to exhibit symptoms of stress, it's a good time to reward it with a treat, end playtime and give it time to settle down.

Many traditional pet owners point to the almost human personalities of their dogs and cats. The same is true with chinchillas. Each animal, regardless of how they are trained and raised, will develop

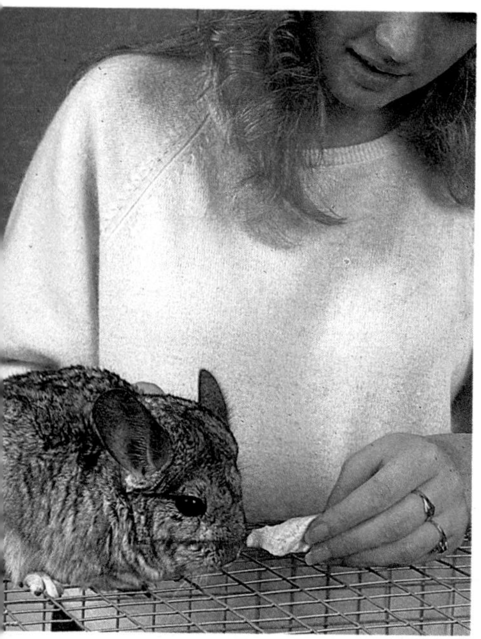

The reward system works equally as well for a chinchilla as for a dog. To offset the possible effect of too many treats on the nutrition of your pet, reduce the regular ration.

its own unique personality. Some enjoy the cuddling and scratching. Others want to explore and chew while still another will not want to be played with at all. If you have more than one pet chinchilla these differences will be more evident and you should make considerations for each one. If you have the opportunity, you should observe any chinchilla you are planning to buy before you take it home. If it has spent any amount of time in the pet shop, its personality traits will already be established. By watching it and, if the pet shop owner allows it, picking it up before making it your own, you can determine if its individual personality is what you are looking for in a pet.

There are advantages and disadvantages of acquiring a pet chinchilla at different ages. How old and mature your pet is when you begin training it makes a difference. You should remember how mature it is when getting acquainted. Newborn chinchillas are very frightened when caught and held, especially those that are less than three weeks old. It will take its lead from its mother and possibly sit on your hand and chew and nibble on it if that's what it sees its mother doing. You really should not try to lift these young kits out of their cage at this time in their lives.

The attitude will probably change once the kit comes close to weaning. By this time they should be willing to come out of their cage, since their sense of curiosity has developed by this point. They will still try to frantically get away and their attention span for any single activity will be extremely short. They will even interrupt their own feeding to run off to taste and examine something else that's caught their eye. Don't be fearful of trying to pet and touch these younger animals. The more contact they have with humans, the quicker they become used to having them around. If they are familiar with you, they will be more ready to have you pick them up and play with them when they are older. Chinchillas who have weaned tend to be a bit more settled. Their confidence has developed and they are much easier to train as pets.

Of course chew blocks and mini-bales can be delightful playthings as well as useful items to ensure the animal's well-being. Playing with these things in the cage with the animal or just observing them play alone is one of the joys of having a chinchilla live in your house. The same is true with watching them enjoy their frequent dust baths. The frantic spinning, twisting, tossing and turning is a constant source of delight and joy for both the chinchilla

Chew sticks, if desired, are safe to offer your chinchilla. They are generally intended for small mammals like hamsters, guinea pigs, gerbils, rats, and mice.

and its owners, be they young or old. While the care and keeping of a chinchilla is an important responsibility, maintaining a sense of "play" while performing these chores enhances the delight of pet ownership.

Tender loving care is also an important part of owning any pet. The chinchilla gained its worldwide fame because of its beautiful and unique fur. Caring for this luxurious coat will provide you with additional close hours with your pet chinchilla. You'll be able to maintain the animal's beauty while becoming closer to your pet as well. This kind of grooming care will also increase the animal's trust towards you too.

Since they are naturally clean and odor free, chinchillas are very easy to keep clean. Their thick fur keeps out insects and other odor-causing parasites. Chinchillas shed their coats approximately every three months. It is not surprising to find balls of loose hair in their cages from time to time. You'll also notice this shedding appearing as uneven fur growth down the animal's back. Their new coats begin their growth at the animal's neck line and move down the back and down the tail. The line formed where the new hair pushes up through the old is known as the chinchilla's priming line. You may not be able to detect such a line on your pet since each animal primes at

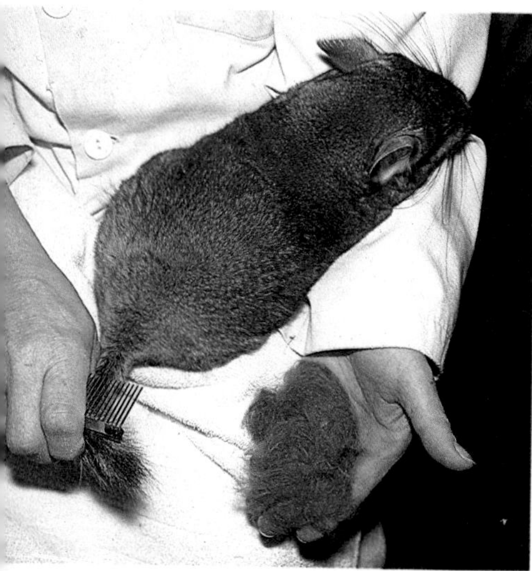

The ball of hair shown was removed by combing. Left uncombed, the loose hair will fall off naturally and can get blown away or caught in parts of the cage, creating an unsightly appearance.

Appearance of a chinchilla after grooming. The fur looks even, as if sheared, when all the loose hairs are combed out.

different rates. Some look as if they have loose hair across their entire bodies, while others have a completely invisible priming line. Some chinchillas will retain this unlined coat for three weeks or more before the new growth begins anew. Still others begin growing a new coat before the old priming line has disappeared down on the tail. Fur ranchers consider the animal's coat to be in perfect condition when the line reaches the tail. Shedding occurs just ahead of the slowly moving mark. When new fur growth reaches the tail, the animal is said to be in prime, and its fur is in the best possible condition. A chinchilla will remain like that for several weeks and then begin to grow all over again.

Both genetic factors and weather conditions come into play regarding an individual animal's priming cycle, and fur ranchers depend on an animal's cycle when selecting their breeding stock. A pet owner's concerns are for the appearance of the animal.

Since your animal lives in a cage, its shed fur will not be blown away by the winds of the world. To aid in both maintaining the cleanliness of the animal's environment and the attractive appearance of the animal, chinchillas require an occasional combing to remove old fur. It is not a necessity for the animal's well-being since their old fur will eventually work its way loose on its own. By regular combings, usually just *prior* to a dust bath, the owner will not have fluffy balls of fur floating all around the cage and the immediate area. The animal will also look a whole lot better after a good combing.

Combing before a dust bath allows the chinchilla's fur to separate so that the dust can penetrate better. You should avoid combing after the dust bath since any dust not completely shaken out by the animal

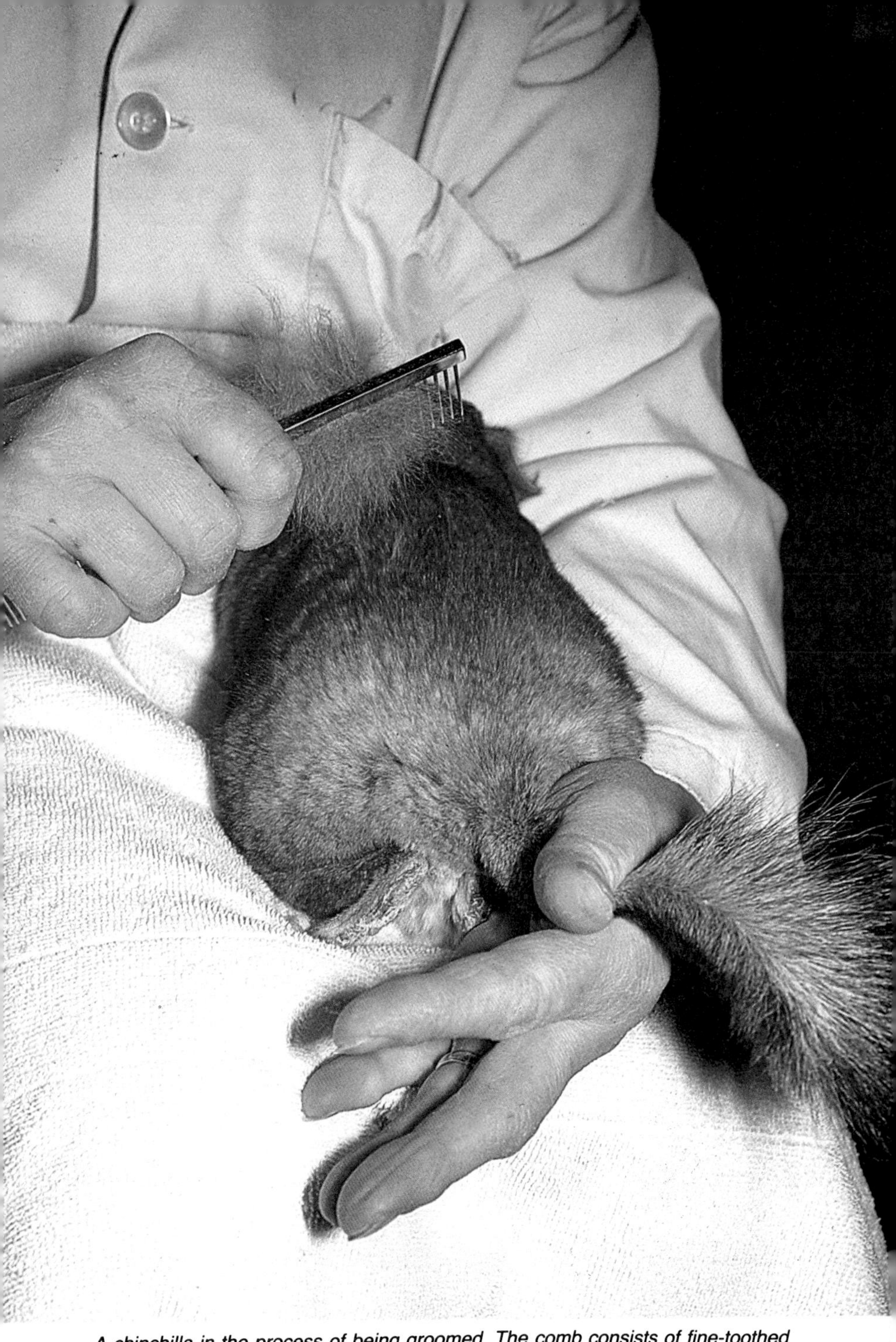

A chinchilla in the process of being groomed. The comb consists of fine-toothed and wide-toothed sections, both of them are with rounded teeth.

will catch on the comb and cause good fur to be pulled out. This will make the animal look worse than when you started and it will cause discomfort to it as well. In fact, it's better to wait a few days, giving the excess dust time to fall out of the animal's thick fur.

You'll need two varieties of combs to do a good job: a rounded edge wide tooth comb and a rounded edge fine tooth comb. Both varieties are readily available at your pet store. There are specific "chinchilla combs" available as well, but these are usually sold only in sets of three, including a pelt comb, which is not needed by a pet owner. It's probably best to buy the two required combs separately. You can groom the animal either on a counter top or on your lap covered by a soft towel, whichever is more comfortable for you and your pet. Beginning with the wide tooth comb, lift and separate small sections of the fur starting at the tail and working your way towards the animal's neck.

A dark, almost black, mutation of chinchilla. White chinchillas are available but considered unsatisfactory as a fur breed.

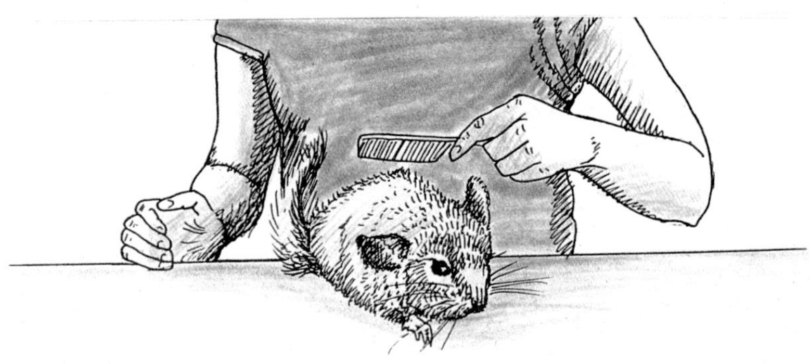

Be sure to restrain your chinchilla at all times while grooming.

A chinchilla photographed with the dust bath material still clinging to the fur. However, with a few shakes, all the particles laden with grime will fall back to the tray.

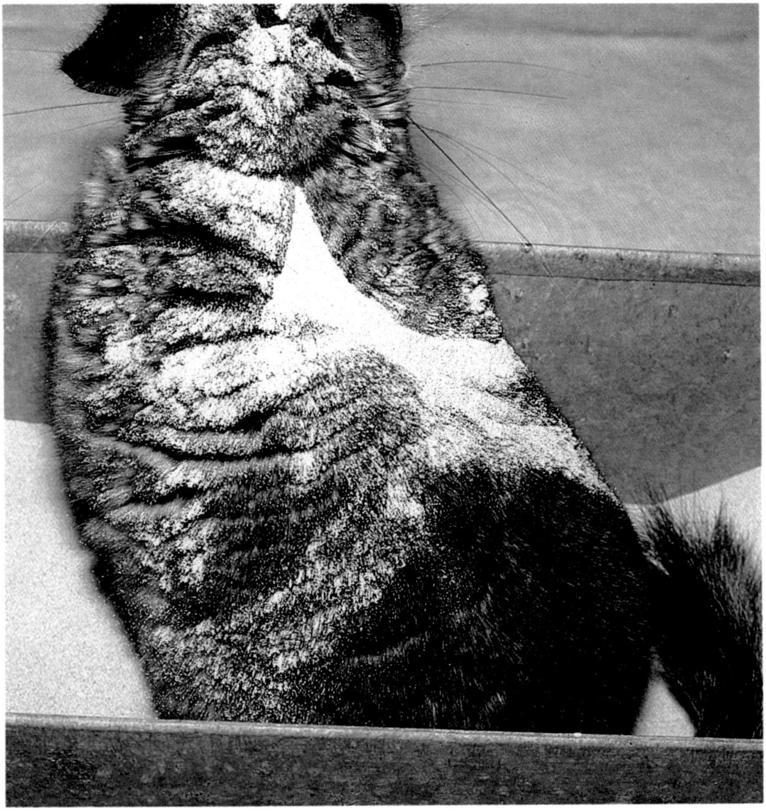

Do all of its back and sides this way and don't worry about the underfur. You'll probably notice marks that this separating action makes on the fur, but they will disappear once the animal gives itself a good shake or with normal active movement.

The fine tooth comb is then used to further separate the hairs and remove any left over loose fur. The animals enjoy this grooming session, especially when you are working over the areas where they normally like being scratched such as behind the ears and under the chin and neck. They might wriggle when you comb them across the back. Most small animals do not like to be combed here. However, if you alternate from the pleasurable areas and then again to the back, they will probably become used to enjoying the entire procedure.

Sometimes the animal's bushy tail will become stained or too long in appearance. If you're careful to clip only the hairs and not the tail itself, this can be groomed as well. Use a sharp pair of scissors and, carefully straightening the hairs with your fingers away from the body, you can snip the extra-long or stained hair off. You'll be able to distinguish tail from hair with your fingers. As long as you keep your fingers between the tail and the scissors, you won't harm the animal. Be sure not to loudly "snip" the scissors. This cutting sound tends to frighten the animal. If you do it slowly, there will be no detectable sudden sound and the animal will not struggle or jump if

For a neat appearance, tail hair can be trimmed off. Be sure to use a sharp pair of scissors and always be aware where the tip of the tail is situated.

properly restrained.

Remember that these animals have a long history in the wild. They enjoy the out of doors as long as the weather remains within parameters they can endure. Unexpected loud noises will make them bolt for a good hiding place, so make certain your outside play area is fenced in. If they escape outside, their natural outdoors instincts will take over and you'll probably never see them again. They will not come scampering home like a cat or a dog.

Outside time is *playing* time. There are too many interesting distractions for your pet outside to think that they will pay attention to any training you might attempt. If you want to maintain training, do so inside.

If you want to play with your chinchilla outdoors, be certain it does not get over-heated. If it stops playing and wants to lie down, or if it starts to breathe heavy and become flushed around the ears, take it back inside.

Trained at an early age, a pet chinchilla can survive to maturity and offer its keeper great pleasure and satisfaction for several years.

Suggested Reading

CHINCHILLAS AS A PROFITABLE HOBBY
By Gerhard Schreiber
PS-852
Hardcover, 5½ × 8½″
160 pages, 65 photos

As author Gerhard Schreiber points out in this detailed and explicit round-up of good advice and highly practical recommendations, breeding chinchillas requires patience, persistence, and perseverance. It also of course requires a good deal of knowledge, and this book—based on the observations and research of author Schreiber and other successful European breeders—provides that knowledge. Generously illustrated, including many attractive full-color photos.

DISEASES OF CHINCHILLAS
By Professor Dr. Helmut Kraft
PS-851
Hardcover, 6 × 9″; 144 pages
Contains more than 20 full-color photos

This book is considered the best available in Germany, where chinchillas are raised by thousands of hobbyists. The book is written for the serious chinchilla hobbyist, dealer and breeder, and it's so good that it can even be helpful to veterinarians.

BREEDING AND CARING FOR CHINCHILLAS
By Egon Mösslacher
PS-850 ISBN 0-86622-118-2
Hardcover, 5½ × 8½″; 128 pages
Over 40 full-color photos

This book has been designed to be of special value to all of the many new chinchilla owners looking for good information about their pets; it provides all of the information they need to allow them to enjoy their pets to the fullest PLUS valuable sections dealing with the breeding of chinchillas.

ALL ABOUT CHINCHILLAS
By Karen Zeinert
PS-845 ISBN 0-86622-143-3
Hardcover, 128 pages, 5½ x 8″
49 full-color photos, 7 black and white photos

ALL ABOUT CHINCHILLAS presents the "soup to nuts" of chinchilla care in an easy-to-read format garnished with nearly 50 full-color photos. Written by a recognized expert in chinchilla culture and care, the book provides a wealth of concise, no-nonsense advice.

CHINCHILLA HANDBOOK
By Edmund Bickel
PS-853

Probably no one in the world had as much practical experience with chinchillas as the author of this book. His contributions to the art and science of chinchilla management and breeding are enormous. Now English-speaking chinchilla fanciers and breeders have a chance to benefit from Edmund Bickel's vast experience as well, because this book (generously illustrated with full-color photos) is the distillation of over half a century of his experiences with and observations of chinchillas from every commercial standpoint.

Index

CO-042 S

t.f.h.

CHINCHILLAS

A COMPLETE INTRODUCTION

Closeup of a mosaic and a beige chinchilla.